Rosaries Aren't {Just} for Teething

Reflections on Mary by Mothers

Edited by Michele E. Chronister

ISBN: 978-0692434000

This book is dedicated to the women who contributed to this volume. Thank you for taking the time to share these beautiful stories of your own motherhood. Your vocations are such a gift to the Church and to the world!

It is especially dedicated to my own mother, Susan, whose deep love for and devotion to Mary was my first introduction to our Blessed Mother.

Foreword

I have a blue, knotted rosary that I keep in my wallet. It seems like a pious habit, and it comes in handy when I want to pray a rosary with a group. More than that, though, I've found it to be an excellent tool to have on hand for teething babies. The current baby of our family is fast approaching two years old, and—along with that—the appearance of her two year old molars. On more than one occasion, she's covered that rosary with more slobber than I ever thought possible.

I'm fairly confident that Mary would be happy to have a rosary used for teething comfort. She is, after all, our heavenly mother, and also experienced the challenge of comforting a teething baby Jesus, firsthand.

Of course, rosaries are good for praying, too. In the spirit of this two-fold use for rosaries, I hope you'll enjoy this little book.

1

Table of Contents

Introduction

I'm a cradle Catholic, and I've always known Mary. For years, though, I didn't feel particularly connected to her. I didn't feel any sort of emotional attachment to her.

Then, my first daughter was born. With the birth of my little Therese, I began to see Mary in a different light. I felt completely in over my head as a new mother, and I asked Mary to say a lot of prayers for me in those early, sleep-deprived days. The more I began to ask for her intercession, the more she began to make sense to me. She was a mother. I had become a mother. I couldn't understand her before, but now, as a fellow mother, I began to see her as a friend.

The rosary began to take on a new meaning for me, once I became a mother. Jesus wasn't just a snuggly, cute baby that I could peer at through a stable window. He was a *newborn*! He needed to be fed around the clock. He pooped and wet himself. He cried. He was up all hours of the night. Did the shepherds or the wisemen show up just as Jesus had finally drifted off to sleep? I'm sure that the Presentation in the Temple was a joyous occasion, but it must have been nerve-wracking taking Jesus on his first real "outing."

Everything was imbued with new meaning. I knew, I just *knew* that Mary "got it." She knew what I was experiencing as a first time mother.

Mary has been a comfort to me at so many times throughout my motherhood. When I was struggling with infertility before my pregnancy with my second daughter, I often felt comfort knowing that Queen of all Saints was mother to "just one." When I struggled in those last few days of pregnancy, trying not to complain, I thought of that poor, aching mother riding on the back of a donkey. When I struggled with the aching loneliness of suffering from hyperemesis gravidarum during my pregnancies, I thought of Mary, rushing to the side of her cousin, and knew that she would rush to my side, too.

Mary is such a comfort to me as a mother, but so are other mothers. Other mothers help me to feel normal, to know that I am not alone in my various struggles. Other mothers uplift me and encourage me. Other mothers share their funny stories with me, and laugh along when I tell them mine. Other mothers encourage me as I grow in my own vocation as a mother.

I sincerely hope that you have fellow women in your life who uplift you, and that Mary is already a friend to you. If she is, this book will encourage you in your journey.

What I hope most deeply, though, is that if you are feeling lonely and overwhelmed in your journey as a mother, this book may help you to know that you are not alone. I hope that as you read through these reflections on the mysteries of the rosary, you will find comfort in getting to know Mary better, and in meeting some fellow mothers who share your experiences. The women who have written these chapters are all mothers or godmothers, and I hope that this book will be one you turn to again and again, as a source of encouragement, comfort, and hope in your vocation as mother.

Mary, Mother of all Mothers, pray for us!

—Michele E. Chronister

A Mother's Marian Litany

Lord have mercy. *Lord have mercy.*
Christ have mercy. *Christ have mercy.*
Lord have mercy. *Lord have mercy.*

Mary, Our Lady of the Annunciation, *pray for us.*
Mary, Our Lady of Comfort, *pray for us.*
Mary, Mother of God, *pray for us.*
Mary, Cause of our Joy, *pray for us.*
Mary, Mother of All Mothers, *pray for us.*

Mary, Refuge of Sinners, *pray for us.*
Mary, Queen of Families, *pray for us.*
Mary, Seat of Wisdom, *pray for us.*
Mary, Queen of Peace, *pray for us.*
Mary, Mother of the Eucharist, *pray for us.*

Mary, Queen of the Angels, *pray for us.*
Mary, Our Lady of Sorrows, *pray for us.*
Mary, Humble of Heart, *pray for us.*
Mary, Comfort of the Afflicted, *pray for us.*

Mary, Morning Star, *pray for us.*
Mary, Mother Most Admirable, *pray for us.*
Mary, Mother Most Amiable, *pray for us.*
Mary, Virgin Most Faithful, *pray for us.*
Mary, Queen of Heaven and Earth, *pray for us.*

The Joyful Mysteries

In the Joyful Mysteries, we encounter a young woman, new to the vocation of motherhood. We find the first Christian, she who first embraced God become man. Mary's experience has supernatural aspects, to be sure – she is the only one who gives birth to one who is both God and man. But Mary also experiences many of the things that all new mothers experience – the uncertainty, the nervousness, the sleeplessness, the joy. Yet, unlike us, she is a model of trust, trusting in God's loving care for her. We turn to her, to teach us how to give God our own trusting fiat.

The First Joyful Mystery
The Annunciation
Mary Frances Moen

If only I could have a love like hers, and so die to my earthly plans in order to completely give myself to a life of motherhood.

I need Mary's loving prayers more than ever before. Her dear Son tells me to learn from the way the wildflowers grow, to trust in him, and to follow his way. But my anxious heart struggles to gaze heavenward. See, the plans God has for me are not the plans that I have for myself. Discipleship is certainly on the list, but my 10-year plan also includes selfish desires, such as: comfort, fame, fortune, security, and simple answers.

This child growing inside of me was always a part of the plan. But now I'm coming to realize that this little one doesn't fit the agenda as well as I had hoped. No longer am I comfortable, and no longer can I strive for fame without considering the impact on this little life. This child will cost me the fortune that I seek, and as I prepare for his or her birth, I am realizing that security and simple answers are rarely found.

The number of days grows smaller, and soon this babe will be in my arms. He or she will depend on me for every need. All that I have planned will be gone, and all that God has planned will soon be swaddled up before me, yearning to be loved. I am unsure and afraid.

I turn to my sweet Mother, because I know that she was once troubled, too. For the angel told her, "Be not afraid." He announced to her that the impossible was possible with God. A virgin was to become a mother. A woman was to give birth to the Son of God.

She was told that the King of the Universe would soon be swaddled up before her, yearning to be loved.

Rather than respond in fear, her perfect faith embraced this plan as better than anything she'd ever dreamed of. Mary's pure heart, still in the same posture of obedience it was in the moment she was immaculately conceived, assented to the Will proposed by Gabriel. It did not calculate how many trials, difficulties, and sorrows such a task would bring about. Nor did it take time to think about the costs and benefits of such a mission. No, her heart responded almost immediately "yes." A simple "yes," to the Father in Heaven who makes all things good.

God is too loving to laugh at our plans. Rather than shake his head at us with a condescending grin, he mercifully offers us something better. Mary's faith in the Father allowed her to fully and freely embrace this "something better," this gift to be given, this joy that she was made for.

I turn to my Blessed Mother, for I know that her fiat was made possible through an abandonment to Divine Providence.

She was ready to say "yes" to God, because she had already placed her trust in him. Her hope was in him, and in him alone.

She may have been surprised at the angel's request. Surprised out of humility, that is, for Mary was chosen from all women. The request itself came as no surprise to her, though. To her it was the most natural thing in the world for a just and loving God to fulfill what was promised. She had abandoned all earthly desires to this promise long ago, and it was this hope that opened her heart in gratitude to the challenge of God's will.

Surely this couldn't have been easy for young Mary, for even those who had hope in God would not have understood what He was doing through her. Her betrothed, her family, her community—how could they have been expected to believe in the bewildering event that took place between Mary and the angel? As a woman abandoned to the Providence of God, this was not her concern. She surrendered to none other than the

Creator, and so she assented to His will with no thought of herself outside of what would be good for all of His creation.

I turn to this dear Mother, for I know it was her silence that led to the silent night of the Nativity. Her obedience in faith, and her abandonment to hope were made possible by a death to self for love of him.

Before her Son showed us how to lay down our lives, Mary laid hers down before the Father. Her soul was quiet, not distracted by earthly cares and desires. She was immaculately dead to herself, allowing the Creator to fill her with His grace. She lived for God and others as a handmaid, and this prepared her for her assent to life as a perfect tabernacle, a mother to the Victor over sin.

In quietly dying to herself, Mary was able to accept all that was needed in order to care for the Christ child. She was able to accept all that was needed to be present to him, even in his journey to Calvary. She was able to give Jesus every bit of love that he needed in order to fulfill his redeeming mission.

If only I could have a faith like hers, and sincerely believe that God is offering me something better by entrusting me with the gift of new life.

If only I could have a hope like hers, and abandon all of myself to the will of the Father, who only wants good things for me.

If only I could have a love like hers, and so die to my earthly plans in order to give myself completely to a life of motherhood.

And so I turn to Mary, because I know that I can have the faith, hope, and love that made her response to the angel's annunciation possible. In fact, it is through her grace-filled assent that this grace is now made available to me.

So it is through my heavenly Mother's powerful intercession that I ask for the grace to be like her, and love God's little plan growing inside of me.

Mary, Our Lady of the Annunciation, pray for us.

The Second Joyful Mystery
The Visitation
Haley Stewart

*That moment of intimate connection and love is
an image of the Visitation to me.*

God is wonderfully *strange*. He is *surprising*. To save the world
from sin, God does the utterly unexpected. He, God himself,
takes on flesh, is born as a helpless human infant in a barn
amidst all of our muck and dirt. He is made great in the small.
He is glorified in the weak. He turns all our expectations upside
down.

The story of the Visitation highlights some of the most
beautifully surprising truths about our mysterious, strange God.
We have Mary, a human woman whose finite womb holds the

infinite God of the cosmos. God himself chose to be incarnate, made into flesh, from this woman. Stop and think of it! God chose that his flesh would be formed from the DNA of a woman in a small town in a far off corner of the world. And not only does he choose this woman, he *asks*. He does not dictate to her what will be, he asks if she will participate in the redemption of the world. After she gives her revolutionary *"Fiat,"* her earth-shattering "yes" that redeems Eve's "no," she visits her aged and barren cousin, Elizabeth.

Elizabeth's shocking late-in-life pregnancy would be a sign that everything the angel Gabriel revealed about Mary's own miraculous pregnancy was true. After the excruciating pain of infertility that Elizabeth and her husband Zechariah had suffered, when all hope seemed lost and they too old to conceive—a miracle! A strange and beautiful unexpected answer to years of heart-wrenching prayers for a baby. So surprising was this, that when Gabriel tells Zechariah of his wife's pregnancy, Zechariah doesn't believe it could be true!

But it *was* true. Elizabeth conceived. And Mary journeyed to be with her cousin—two women carrying miracles in their wombs. I love imagining that moment when the Mary and Elizabeth see each other. When I was pregnant with my first child, we were living across the country from extended family. I was in the third trimester before we had a chance to visit our hometown. I vividly remember stepping out of the car after pulling into my parents' driveway and running to hug my mom. When she saw me, belly full with her first grandchild, she burst into happy tears. I won't ever forget that hug. That moment of intimate connection and love is an image of the Visitation to me.

Did Elizabeth know Mary would be coming, or was it a surprise visit? Was Mary visibly pregnant, or did Elizabeth just *know* of the treasure hidden in her womb?

I imagine Elizabeth watching from the doorway as Mary approached and running out to meet her. I imagine the two women hugging and then holding each other's bellies in wonder, unable to hold back tears of awe. And in that moment, that space is the most important spot on the face of the earth—in the entire cosmos. The universe spins around two women in a small town in the middle of nowhere. Not queens commanding armies of men. Not anyone the world around them would distinguish as special or powerful. But two women carrying miracles in their wombs.

Mary sees with her own eyes the miracle of Elizabeth's growing belly and Elizabeth says, *"Blessed are you among women! And blessed is the fruit of your womb."* As she hears Mary's greeting, Elizabeth feels St. John the Baptist leap for joy. Both Jesus and his Mother are inches away. Nothing more important was happening anywhere on earth.

How strange and how wonderful! Did tears stream from their faces at the goodness of our God? A child for the barren woman. A savior for the suffering world. God himself and the forerunner of his grace in St. John the Baptist, contained in the wombs of seemingly ordinary women. What a strange and miraculous God we serve!

Sometimes I think that if I was just given a miracle like Elizabeth, I would carry it in my heart like she carried her baby and I would never forget the glory of God. But the truth is, I *have* been given a miracle. I have been given a thousand miracles. From the miraculous grace of existence given to us by God, to His scandalous redemption of all my sin on the Cross, to the million tiny miracles that are woven through each of my days. Each of my babies is a miracle. The love of my husband is miraculous. Every Mass we witness the miracle of Heaven reaching down to Earth in the Blessed Sacrament. Miracles surround me through the everydayness of life and the suffering and the joys. I should carry the miracle of God's love in my heart tenderly and thoughtfully like a precious child in my womb, remembering that the earth I walk on has been touched by heaven. That God himself has walked with us in the middle of history, because despite all of our failures He *loves* us, enough to die so that we might *live*.

Inspired by the Visitation, let us bring the knowledge and hope of Christ into every pocket of our lives. Let us nurture loving community with other women, knowing that although we don't physically carry God in our wombs, we consume his Body in the Eucharist and He lives within us. The image of God is imprinted on every human soul. We are to follow in Mary's footsteps, willing to be God-bearers, to have Our Lord dwell within us, to seek to give Christ flesh by our lives so that He is incarnate in us.

Let us model the tender love between Elizabeth and Mary. Let us fill our communities with that love founded on our living hope, Christ Our Lord. A hope that does not despair when all is dark, even in the face of death. Let us remember that our God is He who gives the gift of new life, even when that dream has been long-abandoned. Let us remember that triumph in the face of inevitable defeat is the mark of God's work. He can turn a crucifixion into a victory. He can save the world with suffering, death, and indomitable love. Let us share the love that glories in the strange miracle of God's mercy. When all hope is lost, let us remember that through two women in the middle of nowhere, God stepped into history and saved us with his unexpected and unceasing love.

Mary, Our Lady of Comfort, pray for us.

The Third Joyful Mystery
The Nativity of Our Lord

Jenny Uebbing

I couldn't believe that this surprise pregnancy was going to culminate with a Christmas day delivery, and I had to laugh because honestly, who but God could have planned such a thing?

I like to think that my most recent pregnancy was the most Marian thing I've ever done in my life. In the spring of 2013 my husband Dave and I were pleasantly surprised and more than a little overwhelmed to find out we were pregnant with our daughter, Genevieve, when her two older brothers were not-quite-one and two-years-old, respectively.

Living in a foreign country, mostly (but not entirely) friendless, and utterly overwhelmed by the complexities of daily

31

living with a language barrier and an utter dearth of convenient, child-friendly resources, I fell to my metaphorical knees in wonder that this particular moment in time was one when God saw fit to send us another little life.

As practicing Catholics who use NFP to understand our fertility, we were confident that God would not send a child during the month in question, but we pledged openness to life when we made our marriage vows, and so that openness extends even to lives planned entirely by God. Evie's life was simply and utterly His idea.

As the spring turned into summer and my belly grew rounder with this mysterious little person, an Italian obstetrician gave us a glimpse into my womb, and a due date: December 25th. I couldn't believe that this surprise pregnancy was going to culminate with a Christmas day delivery, and I had to laugh because honestly, who but God could have planned such a thing? Once the novelty of a *bambino de Natale* wore off, I began to quietly freak out about the logistics of the entire situation. We lived in Rome, just blocks from the Vatican, in a fourth-story walkup apartment with marble floors and a perilous balcony which daily gave me mini heart attacks as my toddlers tested their limits and I hung laundry. We had no car, no medical insurance, and no idea what it would be like trying to get to the hospital in the middle of the night during the Christmas season. Would cabs even be running? Would the hospitals shut down, as Italian entities are wont to do, during a major holiday? Would I sufficiently master the language to be able to summon an anesthesiologist to my non-private (horror of horrors) birthing room when the moment came?

Overwhelmed by fear and details, I plunged into the study of ex-pat blogs and online message boards, combing the internet for other women who had lived what I was experiencing. I ruthlessly grilled my Italian mamma friends on their own delivery experiences, and I honed my translation skills, pouring over hospital reviews and brochures. It was ridiculous, but it felt so essential to me. There were so many unknowns and so many variables outside my control—I've never felt so helpless.

If only I had taken the Marian symbolism of my situation to heart and trusted Him, from the very beginning of this pregnancy. Looking back now I can see His providence so clearly, His fingerprints covering every moment of my maternal journey.

The shocking heat of the Roman summer set in and my boys and I adopted a minimalist wardrobe, spending our early mornings and late nights outside in the parks and piazzas that came to life after the sun had set. As I filled and re-filled their Ikea infant bathtub with cool water for them to splash in during the hottest hours of the day, I nearly despaired at the thought of mothering three small children in our tiny, blessedly air-conditioned apartment. Surely He would provide though, my unflagging husband would reassure me in the evenings as we sat on the balcony with cool glasses of bubbly prosecco, watching the lights of St. Peter's illuminate the dome as night fell. Dave never questioned God's timing or His providence for us—he was, and is, my St. Joseph. Quiet, tireless, and utterly committed to doing God's will.

Then, while on a long-awaited visit home to the U.S. to visit family and friends and Super Target, Dave received a job offer back in our hometown. It was, as his current boss pointed out, an offer he couldn't refuse.

And just like that we were packing again, only nine months after arriving in Italy. As we shed belongings and said our goodbyes to Rome I was pinching myself in disbelief; all my fears and anxieties of the past six months simply melted away. We were going home. This baby was going to be born in a place I knew and loved, and I would be surrounded by friends and family.

I sobbed with relief as we boarded the plane bound for Dublin-then-Denver, saving a few tears for the friends we'd leave behind and the beauty we'd seen over that past not-quite-year, but mostly just relief. I felt acutely that God had heard my cry and that He had utterly and magnificently provided for me, in His own time and in a way so unfathomably greater than anything I could have imagined.

Four months after we arrived home, our little bundle of Christmas joy arrived ten days early, filling the end of Advent with diapers and late night feedings rather than expectant hope. I spent that Christmas not in a cold, unfamiliar hospital room surrounded by strangers, but in my parents' house, holding my newborn daughter and praising God that His plans are always better than mine, and the stories He writes are always more interesting.

So while I never had to mount a donkey and make haste for the city of my husband's ancestors, my surprising Christmas pregnancy forged a connection with Our Lady and her willingness to accept and to receive from the Lord every good thing. Especially that best Thing, who turned out to be a Person, the source of all joy.

Mary, Mother of God, pray for us.

The Fourth Joyful Mystery
The Presentation in the Temple
Michele E. Chronister

Mary and Jesus, from the beginning, show us that we needn't be afraid of that suffering. We don't need to shy away from the less-than-ideal reality of motherhood in our world.

I'm sure that I wasn't the only first-time mother to have great expectations for pregnancy. One of my predictions was that I would *not* suffer from morning sickness. Unfortunately, it quickly became clear that I am one of those rare women who suffers from hyperemesis gravidarum during pregnancy, a condition resulting in severe nausea and/or vomiting for a large portion of a woman's pregnancy. My experience of pregnancy was nothing like what I thought it would be, and I was eager to deliver my first daughter.

I knew that there was a possibility that I might suffer from postpartum depression, but (expectations, expectations) I was very hopeful that I would be spared. I was blindsided by how *difficult* motherhood was, and I suffered from terrible baby blues, and later from postpartum depression.

Yet, it was the loneliness that made my pregnancy and postpartum time most difficult. I was supported by family, and friends—but I knew no one who had had an experience like mine with pregnancy. I felt so alone, and like such a terrible failure.

The moment that shifted my view of motherhood was when the priest poured holy water over my daughter's head and said, "I baptize you in the name of the Father, and of the Son, and of the Holy Spirit." Suddenly, my motherhood made sense. The suffering seemed like nothing in light of the fact that *my child had just become a member of the Church*. She could call

God, "Father" and Mary, "Mother." She could live forever, in heaven, with all the saints and angels. She could even *be* a saint.

Throughout all of this, I found myself thinking again and again of the Blessed Mother, and her experience as a mother. Can you imagine what her expectations of motherhood would have been, given her upbringing? There were wives and mothers all around Mary. Babies were probably a natural part of the landscape. And marriage. . . marriage always came first. After that, a pregnancy would follow—a time of preparation where a woman would be surrounded by her mother and other women, all eagerly anticipating the birth of the child. When her time came to deliver, she would be in the competent hands of the women of her family, who would tenderly care for her and her new baby. After the birth of the child, the father—glowing with pride—would be invited to meet his little son or daughter.

What was Mary's experience? First, a betrothal, followed by a visit from an angel asking her to bear the Son of God. Then, she was off to visit a cousin, and returned to a fiancé who was less than thrilled with her newly pregnant state. She faced the danger of being stoned, and the reality of being ostracized. Then, Mary and her new husband found themselves traveling the long distance to a strange place while she was in *her third trimester of pregnancy.* She gave birth to a baby all alone—no mother, no cousins, no kinswomen. There was no one there to help her latch on her baby for that first breastfeeding session. Her husband, bless his heart, surely tried his best, but the care of a man isn't the same as the care of a fellow woman in these types of situations.

So, by the time Mary, Joseph, and Jesus were heading off to Jerusalem for the Presentation in the Temple, Mary was probably needing a little encouragement. She probably was excited to show off Jesus to anyone and everyone who would admire him. Maybe she hoped to befriend some other young mothers, also arriving for their purification and the presentation of their first sons. *Finally*, Mary would get to have a typical new mother experience—presenting her child in the temple, with her husband glowing with pride at her side.

When an older man approached them, smiling and joy-filled, gesturing to her son, Mary must have been bursting with her own share of joy. Remember, she knew that this baby was special. Not only was she happy for them to admire *her child*, but she surely must have been excited to bring the Messiah to others.

The older man took the child into his arms, probably cooing the sweet sounds that grandparents always seem to know how to make for babies. But then, he spoke. And what was that? A *sword* would pierce her heart? Her mother's heart?

Now, were I Mary, you can bet I would have had a few choice words for God at this point. Jesus was her first (and only) baby. Couldn't she experience just a little normalcy? Couldn't she have just been allowed to cuddle her baby in her own home, instead of a stable? Couldn't she have been pampered and cared for, as all new mothers crave?

Thankfully, Mary was not me. Mary was not selfish. She knew a secret that I'm still learning, and that most of us with birth plans and baby registries and epidurals and birthing tubs and doulas forget. Motherhood is our *vocation.* Yes, those babies bring us much pleasure, but motherhood isn't just about our own pleasure. It is a sharing in the self-giving love of God. It is also a sharing in the suffering of the cross. No matter how much we try to control our motherhood, no matter how much we crave that "perfect" experience, we cannot force our situation to be something other than it is. We are fallen people, living in a fallen world, and things just *aren't perfect* in this world.

I'm willing to bet that my experience of motherhood is not unique. Maybe some of the particulars are unique to me, but there are many women who face unexpected suffering and difficulty in pregnancy, labor, delivery, and the postpartum period. Many women face *far greater* suffering than I do during pregnancy. Many women are disappointed by aspects of the process of becoming a mother.

The saints are one of the greatest consolations in my life. In my motherhood, Mary and her story have been among my greatest comforts. Yes, my nausea during pregnancy is pretty awful. Yes, postpartum depression is far from the ideal. But, when my sufferings are united to those of Christ on the cross, I become an integral part of God's plan. I become a part of bringing a new soul into the world. I am given the chance to birth a beautiful little person who becomes an adopted child of God, a brother or a sister to Mary's Son.

What Mary teaches us about motherhood is counter-cultural. It goes against everything that we are told today about motherhood. There is no "perfect" pregnancy/birthing experience/babymoon. There is the reality of the challenges of pregnancy, infertility or super-fertility, painful labor and delivery, and obstacles that stand in the way of a mother bonding with her baby the way she'd like. Were it not for Mary and her baby, it would be enough to make us despair.

But Mary and Jesus, from the beginning, show us that we needn't be afraid of that suffering. We don't need to shy away from the less-than-ideal reality of motherhood in our world. Our motherhood, when accepted as a gift from God, has eternal meaning. It is a gift that not even a sword, piercing the heart, can shatter. Mary gives us hope, so much hope, that motherhood is about more than this world tells us. It is about love, true love. And true love may lead to pain, but it also is a cause for joy.

Mary, Cause of our Joy, pray for us.

The Fifth Joyful Mystery
The Finding in the Temple
Caitlyn Buttaci

This act brings a heightened importance to what we do as mothers. If even Our Lord insisted on ordered home life, even more so do our own children.

It's hard to imagine losing a child while traveling, let alone spending three days trying to find him. The fear and worry that must have been racing through Mary and Joseph's hearts over those three days is incomprehensible. When they found him and he casually said to Mary, "Why were you looking for me? Did you not know I would be about my Father's business?" she must have been astounded. Here was her son, recognizing his divinity at such a young age. She had to have thought that his time had come. However, the Gospel tells us that he then went home with his parents, Mary and Joseph, and was obedient to them until he began his public ministry roughly twenty years later.

Mary never planned on being a mother. It was to her great surprise that she was told she would give birth to the Son of God. While I have led a vastly different life than Mary did, I too was not always convinced that motherhood was the life for me. When I was young, I often thought of being a religious sister. The calling intrigued me, as it seemed to be the only way I could live a holy life. I fought with discernment over the course of a few years, before it became clear to me that there is a call to holiness in *every* vocation. Slowly, it became evident that I was called to be a wife and mother.

A few years later, as I was preparing to become a mother for the first time, I imagined raising good, holy children in the faith. I thought of teaching them to read, taking them on vacations, sharing holiday traditions with them—all of the fun aspects of motherhood. I could not have understood the ways in which being a mother could lead me to holiness. In the past it had seemed easy to obey God's will and live the life of wife and mother. I never thought through the mundane aspects of the vocation. I could not have known how frustrating it would be to have a toddler ask ten times in a row if his piece of cheese is, in fact, a piece of cheese. I had no idea that babies, as cute as they are, come with an onslaught of postpartum hormones and emotions. I never imagined struggling to understand just what my child wants as he is throwing a tantrum on the floor, unable to calm down. I find motherhood trying and difficult. I often do not like aspects of it, and I find it hard to give fully of myself in both body and spirit as a wife and mother. It is a demanding life and one that often seems small and thankless.

A good friend of mine once told me that we shouldn't diminish our vocation as mothers. These children need us in ways we cannot understand. It's easy to hem and haw our way through these sleepless nights. Some nights we can't manage anything else. They are trying nights but they are the nights when we are most called to be mothers. To the children, we are the ones who can comfort them back to sleep and banish the monsters from under the bed. Mother Teresa may have been a missionary to the poor but we are missionaries to our children. It may sometimes seem insignificant to us, but to them it is their whole world.

I'm reminded of a night when I found myself caring for our newborn daughter. She was around three months old and still waking up a few times at night. As I was nursing her back to sleep, I heard the two-year-old crying at his door. He does not often wake up at night, so I was more than a little surprised. I woke my husband up, who went in to comfort him. As my husband tried to leave our son's room a little while later, he started crying again. The baby was back asleep, so I slipped out of bed and went to take over on toddler duty. Less than a couple of hours later, my husband was at the door telling me the baby was awake again. So, dad took over for the toddler again while I shimmied out of one child's bed and back to the other's. Sure enough, we traded places at least one more time before the alarm started going off and it was time to start a new day.

In the morning, I had to laugh at the absurdity of the situation. This was certainly not how I envisioned motherhood to be, but there I was. I had two choices: I could spend the night huffing around complaining about my children being horrible sleepers or I could simply accept the situation I was given and serve my children.

On the mornings after those sleepless nights, we pour an extra cup of coffee, we hug our babies (who have little concept of the lack of sleep they have inflicted upon us), and we plug through yet another day. While, like Mary and Joseph, we may not always understand the significance of our children's antics, we should carry on about our days, trusting that what we're doing is pleasing to God.

God willed that His only Son, perfect as He is, submit Himself to be obedient to His earthly parents. This act brings a heightened importance to what we do as mothers. If even Our Lord insisted on ordered home life, even more so do our own children. So, just as Mary and Joseph obeyed the Father's will by providing Jesus a home within which He could grow in "wisdom and age and favor" (Luke 2:52), we should strive to do the same for our own families. We can pray that our Blessed Mother, who is our model in motherhood, aid us with grace to do so.

Mary, Mother of All Mothers, pray for us.

The Luminous Mysteries

In the Luminous Mysteries, Mary gives us the perfect example of how to strike a balance in parenting our growing children; she steps back and allows God's will to be done in the life of her Son, and also allows God to continue to work in her. Mary is the first disciple. She is the first to give God her most perfect "yes," and she is the first to follow the way of her Son. She gives all mothers an example of what it means to truly follow Christ.

The First Luminous Mystery
The Baptism in the Jordan
Cari Donaldson

Did she know that this moment marked the end of the hidden life she'd shared with her Son, and that from that point forward, every step took Him closer and closer to the Cross?

In my wilderness years, I did not often trouble myself with logic or consistency. At least not in my theological considerations. Before I threw my lot in with the Church, the highest good a spiritual truth could hold was that it made me feel good.

The concept of sin, it goes without saying, did not fit that bill.

In the all-you-can-eat junk food buffet that is the New Age movement, sin is rarely given serious consideration, and when it is, it's only to find ways to downplay or sidestep it. So, when I found myself pregnant with my first child, a curious struggle began to play itself out in my heart. On the one hand, I strongly felt the urge to baptize this child in some manner, but on the other hand, my lack of belief in sin or any tenants of Christianity whatsoever made the pull puzzling. Why a baptism? To what end? What did I hope to accomplish with this ritual, and how would it even play out in a non-Christian setting?

The "why" I never much troubled myself with, but the "how" I tackled with enthusiastic high spirits. The family would gather at a local park, I would recite a poem my uncle had once composed for a similar baptism of his oldest child, and my baby would be doused with lake water in a ceremonial dedication of her as a "child of the universe."

There wasn't a trace of mockery in my heart in regards to this. . . *thing* I was planning, but neither was there a good deal of logic. On the day of the baptism, or whatever it really was, I remember bending down to catch some of Lake Kensington in the decorative vase I'd bought for the occasion, and being momentarily troubled that even this, this ritual that I handcrafted to perfectly suit all my spiritual desires, was somehow leaving me with a feeling of emptiness. I quickly brushed the thought away and focused on my beautiful daughter, held in the arms of her godmother. As far as I was concerned, that tiny, perfect baby was pure and perfect and wasn't, nor ever would be, touched by something as dreadful as sin. If this action felt empty, it was because *she* was empty—empty of sin and any inclination towards anything but goodness. She was a child of the universe, untethered and unspoiled—totally free to choose whatever path the search for her own bliss took her down.

A few years later, freshly converted (and with children validly baptized using the Trinitarian formula), I would meditate on the Mystery of Our Lord's Baptism, and shake my head at the ocean of difference that separated that event from the one I concocted for my firstborn child. I would think about Our Lady, and wonder about the play of thought and emotion that moved in her as she watched her child, sinless in fact, and not just maternal sentiment, engage in the actions of a penitent man. How did she keep in check the righteous indignation all mothers feel on behalf of their children—seeing the spotless Child of the Most High engaging in actions that marked Him as a sinner? Did she know that this moment marked the end of the hidden life she'd shared with her Son, and that from that point forward, every step took Him closer and closer to the Cross? If she knew, how did she stop herself from begging Him for more time, even a single day more, where it could just be Mother and Child, the world kept in wait for just a little longer?

When I think of the Baptism of the Lord, it's always the strength of Mary's heart that I ponder. There is a huge gulf between my firstborn's baptism and that of Mary's firstborn, but eventually, our paths will align. My children will grow up, and the hidden lives I've shared with them will be over. They will begin their own public ministry, follow their own vocations, and I will have to share them ever more with the world. They will walk toward their own crosses, and while I may be able to help them shoulder the burden somewhat, I will never be able to fully take it away. They will pay the wages of sin with suffering and their eventual death, just as we all must. Far from a life endlessly pursuing personal comfort and bliss I had once hoped for my firstborn, I had now set my children down a path of discipleship—a path that goes up to, and through, the Cross.

Those times are looming on the horizon, coming ever closer into focus, like the crowds on the banks of the River Jordan. So when I pray the Mystery of the Baptism of Our Lord, I think of my baptism. The Catechism reminds us that through it, the Christian is sacramentally assimilated to Jesus, whose death and resurrection is foreshadowed in his own baptism. But I also think of my children, about the end of our hidden lives together, and about the beginning of their public walk as disciples. Then my heart hurts and my eyes get weepy.

When that happens, I turn my head from the river, and look for Our Lady among the crowds standing watch. I grab for her hand and hold tight, knowing that she will lead my mother's heart through the things to come: all the things that I will have to walk through, and all the ones I will have to watch my children walk through. Despite what I had once foolishly insisted, there *is* sin in the world, and suffering is its companion—to deny this doesn't banish it, no matter how many rituals and ceremonies one makes up to convince the heart otherwise. We will all walk down the path to the Cross, but if we first walked down to that river, the Cross will not be the end.

We go to the water to die, but we come up again with the promise of life everlasting.

Mary, Refuge of Sinners, pray for us.

The Second Luminous Mystery
The Wedding Feast at Cana
Michele E. Chronister

When Mary prayed for the couple in Cana—and when she prays for us—she does so with great love. She is always wanting what is best for us. She prays for us and for our needs with incredible tenderness.

When my husband and I got married, we were brand new graduate students. Our whole marriage has been spent on a fairly tight budget. In the beginning, that used to be a source of stress for me; as time has gone on, it has become a source of grace.

Our entire marriage has been a lesson in learning to trust that God will provide. And the last (almost six) years have been peppered with stories of God's providence. From the very beginning, each step we would take to say "yes" to God, He would honor by giving us what we needed (and often in unexpected ways). We found our first home fairly quickly, with the help of fellow theology graduate students who were renting a beautiful, *affordable* home from an older Catholic couple. My thesis advisor generously gave us some hand-me-down furniture. Our family pulled together and moved all our furniture into our new home, so that we wouldn't have to rent a moving truck or hire movers.

We weren't the kind of couple that was particularly concerned about our wedding reception details. We were very interested in planning the wedding Mass (being a couple of theology students), but we didn't have as much interest in a fancy reception. Nonetheless, we knew we needed to fill out a wedding registry, plan reception details, pick a menu, select invitations, buy a wedding dress and wedding rings, and select our reception venue. No matter how simple of a wedding you want, there are some details that are just unavoidable.

We were planning our wedding during our senior year of college, and we allotted one Friday afternoon to look at reception venues back in my hometown. None of the venues were extravagant by any means, but some were definitely more expensive than others. Our final venue was an old-fashioned, simple, but nice hall, owned by the local Greek Orthodox church. In contrast to the polished, professional woman who showed us around our first venue, an older Greek man unlocked the door for us, and gestured us in. He walked us through the hall, and then said (in his distinctly Greek accent), "So, what do you think? You rent the hall, have beautiful babies, and be very happy!"

Despite that irresistible offer, we told him we'd have to think about it. My parish (the church we were going to be married in) had a daily Mass on Friday evening, so we decided to go to that. After Mass, we stayed in the back pew, praying together. While we were praying, a slow stream of people came in—a few adults and a child—and made their way to the front of the church. The pastor came out, and what quietly and simply unfolded was a convalidation ceremony, a blessing of a marriage that had happened outside of the Church. It was so simple, but it struck right to the heart of what mattered about a wedding. Afterwards, Andrew and I turned to each other and said, "I think we'll take that last church hall for our reception venue." We saw that that inexpensive option was God's beautiful way of providing for us. And do you know what? We have had beautiful children, and we are very happy.

I love the story of the wedding feast at Cana. I love it for the reason that it demonstrates how, if you invite God to be a part of your marriage, he will always provide for you. That has certainly been our experience! Since becoming a mother, though, I appreciate the role that Mary plays in this story.

Mary and Jesus are both at this wedding feast at Cana. Perhaps Mary was friends with the newlyweds and their family.

At any rate, she was attune enough to what was happening at the feast that she knew the moment the wine ran out. And she ran to her Son. She asks Jesus to provide, and at first he protests, "My hour has not yet come." But how does Mary respond? "Do *whatever* he tells you."

And do you know what? Jesus performs His first miracle, changing the water into wine. I never understood this exchange, or Mary's intercessory role in the Church. Theologically, I understood it perfectly. Yet, I didn't think about it too deeply, because I hadn't yet experienced firsthand the role that a mother plays as intercessor for her children.

I am, by far, the "softy" in our family, and our daughters know it. Their dad loves them deeply, but he doesn't have a problem enforcing bedtimes, naptimes, and various rules. I don't have a problem enforcing them either, but I'm also more aware (as the person who is with them all day) of unique situations that may arise that call for exceptions to the rules. As a result, I've sometimes found myself playing the role of "intercessor" in our family.

Our second born was a very colicky baby, with reflux. She bonded with me quickly (as the source of her milk) but with everyone else slowly. Consequently, I was the one who spent the most time with her, and who was most aware of what she needed and what she wanted. She was a very sensitive baby, and had very specific needs. Andrew is definitely a hands-on type of dad, and wanted to do all that he could to help her (and me) through those newborn days. But there were times that he would offer suggestions for how to help Maria calm down or fall asleep— ones that had worked perfectly well for our non-colicky firstborn. We would end up deep in conversation as we tried to figure out if his suggestions would work with Maria. And often, I would be the one gently pleading that we try a more flexible approach. Much of the time, I would win him over to my way of thinking.

Now granted, my intercessory experience is not exactly like Mary's. Neither Andrew nor I are without sin, and our wills are not perfect (or perfectly united). There is always give and take, and many times his fatherly suggestion actually *is* the one that works best. Nevertheless, the experience of effective and gentle pleading for my children, to their father, has given me some insight into the immense love behind Mary's intercession.

When Mary prayed for the couple in Cana—and when she prays for us—she does so with great love. She is always wanting what is best for us. She prays for us and for our needs with incredible tenderness. I know this because I—with all my weakness and frailty and sin—pray for my girls with deep tenderness and love. How much more so must our perfect heavenly mother do this for each of us, her children?

Mary, Queen of Families, pray for us.

The Third Luminous Mystery
The Proclamation of the Kingdom

Katie Busch

Being a mom isn't just about the moments of grace we experience because of our children. It's mostly about, and lived through, the daily grind of parenthood.

Tucked in the middle of the Luminous Mysteries, between sacraments and miracles, is the Proclamation of the Kingdom and Jesus's call to conversion. It's always seemed a bit out of place to me, this wide swath of scripture that's included in this mystery, nested between short moments of grace in the mysteries on either side. It felt almost like a cop out, as if Pope Saint John Paul II, in the midst of enumerating the Luminous Mysteries, thought to himself, "Oh, yeah, all that other stuff Jesus said and did, too." But when I look at it through the lens of my role as mother of my children, its place in the rosary makes perfect sense.

Being a mom isn't just about the moments of grace we experience because of our children. It's mostly about, and lived through, the daily grind of parenthood. It's "all that other stuff" we say and do as parents that doesn't necessarily pop out as anything special or extraordinary, especially when compared to the grace-filled moments of giving birth or baptizing our child or being told "I love you" for the first time. The Proclamation of the Kingdom parallels our daily life as parents, reflecting how we proclaim the Kingdom of God to our children and how we gently call them to a relationship with God.

Jesus proclaimed the Kingdom in two ways, by His teachings and by His actions, and as mothers we do the same for our children. I cannot teach my daughters about God if I only teach them their catechism and leave it at that, no matter how thorough my teaching is. I cannot teach my daughters about

God, either, if I only live according to His directives and don't share the reasons for my actions. There's a Why and a How, and each is not enough without the other.

Where all of this really comes to a head is in the day-to-day life of a mom, although it's not obvious to the casual observer. One of the worst questions I hear from well-meaning friends who don't have children is, "So, besides taking care of the girls, what do you *do*?" It makes my skin crawl. It's like fingernails on a chalkboard. There is no "besides" taking care of my children. That's just it. That's the crux of my vocation and, frankly, the job of being a mother. I'm not simply keeping my children alive and healthy; I'm proclaiming the Kingdom of God to my girls. When I wake them up in the morning with a smile on my face, when I stop my chores to help Mary with an art project or to cuddle Hannah for a nap, when I tell my husband "I love you" before I hang up the phone, when I help Mary light a votive candle at church, when I show Hannah the stained glass image of the Holy Family after mass, even when I'm disciplining one of them, I am teaching my girls about God's love for them and how they can begin to enter into a relationship with Him.

Jesus taught his disciples day in and day out. He often repeated himself or had to come up with yet *another* parable to try to get His point across. How many times did Jesus begin, "The Kingdom of God is like a. . ."? How many times do we as mothers have to explain and re-explain to our children why biting is bad, why they have to obey us, or why Christ died on the cross? These are all ways we call our children to God, and it's a continual conversation that begins at birth and never ends.

Jesus knew that it would take more than sacraments and miraculous moments to lead people to God. It would also require a constant flow of theological conversation and patient love. That is what we mothers are called to share with our children. Our quotidian routines are not just something to kill time between miraculous moments of grace or childhood Sacraments. The Proclamation of the Kingdom is no less important than the Baptism of our Lord, the Wedding at Cana, or the Transfiguration. It ties them together and gives them context. In that same way, how we proclaim the Good News to our children gives context to the more obviously religious moments in their lives.

Something that struck me as I got to know my husband John, was how much my own understanding of God's love was rooted in my understanding of human love. I knew that my parents loved and treasured me as their daughter, and I knew that God loved me even more than they did. As I fell in love with John, though, my frame of reference shifted. Before, I had imagined love on a scale of one to ten, with God's love floating somewhere above ten. But with my love for John the scale suddenly grew a hundredfold, as did my perception of the magnitude of God's love.

This is also how it should be for my children. They will know the love of God because they will have my own example of parental love. They will be able to say, "Mom and Dad love me so much, and God loves me even more!" I proclaim the Kingdom of God to my young girls by giving them a starting point, a baseline, for understanding God's love for them. This doesn't only occur in the big moments of life with children. Rather, it occurs in our day-to-day exchange of love, compassion, and mercy.

Mary, Seat of Wisdom, pray for us.

The Fourth Luminous Mystery
The Transfiguration
Mary Lenaburg

Since the moment of Courtney's first seizure, I had begged, pleaded, whined, complained, and argued with God. But had I ever listened to him?

When I was twenty-five, everything that I thought my life would be changed in the span of an afternoon. My infant daughter was diagnosed with a seizure disorder of unknown origin, cortical blindness and global developmental delay—meaning she would never speak, see, or walk—she would be dependent on me for her daily care for the remainder of her life. Even the length of that life was in dispute. I had gone from being a mom to a caretaker. God had abandoned me. I was alone.

After spending several weeks mourning the future I had lost, I decided I had to *fix it*. I spent the next seven years in and out of doctors' offices all over the U.S., searching for an answer for my daughter. Searching for something that would make her seizures go away.

During those years, I continued to go to Mass (since the nuns had taught me that my not doing so would result in *dire* circumstances) but my personal relationship with God went from hot to cold in the blink of an eye. I went to church out of fear. There was no give and take, no quiet conversations, no friendship between God and me. Because I was angry that God had allowed this to happen, I tried to control every aspect of my world: my daughter's medical prognosis, my son's developing emotional detachment, my husband's everything.

This worked well enough, except for our growing debt, my widening waistline, my son's anger management, and my husband's pornography addiction. Yes, I had everything under control.

In the year 2000, we went on a pilgrimage to Lourdes, France with our daughter. Finally, I was going to get my miracle. God was going to sweep in and my girl would be cured. She would regain her sight and the use of her legs. I would hear the precious words, "I love You, Mom."

I believed, without doubt, that she would be cured. So few children have the opportunity to make the pilgrimage, that when my daughter was chosen I knew God had a miracle planned. Why else would He make it happen? Although my relationship with God was shaky, Courtney's was perfect. He would not let her down.

But when we didn't get the miracle we expected, all my old insecurities rushed back. I was not good enough. I didn't deserve a miracle. I couldn't *fix* her.

But the thing that confused me the most was that He had denied Courtney, who had no sin to stand between her and God.

And that quietly broke my heart.

When we got home from France, I had to adjust to the truth that I would always be her caretaker—the one who changed her diapers, fed her, and deciphered her nonverbal grunts and groans. I would never be the mother who took her to tea, bought her a prom dress, or watched her get married and have a family. This life was here to stay. There'd be no reset button. I would never have the life I had dreamed of.

Then, late one night, my daughter had multiple grand mal seizures which left us both exhausted. Once she fell asleep, I dropped to the ground next to her bed. I felt empty and alone. Sitting there, in the dark, I grabbed the Bible from her dresser and began to read. As I read, my tears blurred every word. In that moment, I poured my heart and soul out to God. I held nothing back. Wave after wave of gut-wrenching grief, lingering guilt and bitter anger flowed like a storm fueled creek running over the hard edges of tree trunks and rocks.

I sat, surrounded by a mountain of wet, white tissues on the cold linoleum floor. I felt raw, exposed, and tender. Like new skin drawn tightly under an old burn.

Once I ran out of tears, I looked down at the open page. Luke 9:29: "While he was praying, the appearance in His face changed and His clothes became dazzling white."

Not impressed since the only white I saw in the room were the mounds of tissues on the floor and the little light bulb of the night light, I kept reading: "Then from a cloud came a voice that said, 'This is my beloved Son, my chosen One, listen to Him.'"

Listen to him.

Since the moment of Courtney's first seizure, I had begged, pleaded, whined, complained, and argued with God. But had I ever listened to him?

A tightness rose in my chest that wasn't from nausea or panic.

Had I listened to him when we'd first received the diagnosis? No.

Had I listened to him during those busy *fix-it* years? No.

Had I listened to him in Lourdes? At that moment, I wasn't sure.

While I can't speak to Courtney's experience in the water, when I was submerged, I heard one word loud and clear. "Acceptance." Now, me being me, sitting on that cold, tissue-laden floor, I felt sure I had listened. I had accepted a life which didn't include a miracle for Courtney. I had accepted and moved on.

As my backside went numb and my arms chilled, I re-read Luke's version of the Transfiguration again. And I began to wonder: *When John, Peter, and James heard God's voice, did they listen? Had they truly comprehended what they had seen and heard? Had I?* In that moment, I thought again about the gift God had given me at Lourdes. While he hadn't given me back the daughter I'd always wanted, he'd given me a word. A word that, up until that moment, I was sure I had understood the meaning of.

Yet as I listened to Courtney's peaceful, even breaths, I contemplated the story. While the Apostles had been given a Divine message, it wasn't until the Holy Spirit arrived about two months later that they truly understood. When I was submerged in the water at Lourdes, didn't the Holy Spirit give me this word of "acceptance"? In a sudden flash of insight, I realized that while I had accepted the daily tasks of caring for Courtney, I had never truly accepted my role in her life or hers in mine.

But now, two months after hearing the word "acceptance," I discovered the truth of the scriptures loud and clear: Jesus is the Chosen Son of God, the Son who accepted his role in God's plan. I finally understood. I had a role in this story too, a role I had not fully understood or accepted. God picked me, of all the women in the world, to be Courtney's mother. That night, God's word completed my transfiguration. It started in Lourdes and ended on a tissue-strewn forty-year-old chipped linoleum floor.

It's been fifteen years since that night, and in that time my life, my heart, my soul was transformed by my love for my daughter, and by my even greater love for the One who had trusted me with the gift of Courtney.

Mary, Queen of Peace, pray for us.

The Fifth Luminous Mystery
The Institution of the Eucharist
Michele E. Chronister

It made sense. It all made sense. . . I had given up my very body for the sake of another.

I have had a tremendous devotion to Jesus in the Eucharist, for as long as I can remember. When I was pregnant with my first child, I remember being aware of how special it was that she and Jesus were both inside of me after Communion. I would pray with her, whispering to her that Jesus was beside her and that He loved her very much.

As both of my girls have grown, I've shared my love for Jesus in the Eucharist with them. It has done my heart good to see how much *they* love Him, too. As babies, they both learned to blow Him kisses, and my youngest is so good at it that she'll blow kisses at any building that even *vaguely* resembles a church. They both fell in love with "Jee" in the Eucharist at a very young age. I know that for me—even with an advanced degree in theology and having taken entire graduate level courses on the Eucharist and the Mass—the reason why I believe in Jesus in the Eucharist is simple. I love Him. My girls don't understand the theological reasons for belief in the Eucharist, but they love Him, too. It has been a tremendous joy to share that love with them.

But the most profound experience that I had with the Eucharist, happened when I was still a brand-new mother. I was in the hospital with Therese, having just given birth to her the day before. I was already so in love with her! Thankfully, she was also an incredibly easy baby to breastfeed, and we spent a lot of time in those first couple of days, cuddled in my hospital bed and nursing. My husband, Andrew, went to Mass at our parish that Saturday evening. When he came back to the hospital that night, he quietly came in and greeted us. Then he whispered to me, "I brought a friend back for you."

Momentarily, I panicked—I was in my hospital gown, unwashed, and had a baby in my arms who would probably want to latch on at any minute. Who had Andrew brought back with him? Then, he reached into his pocket and pulled out a gold pyx. He had brought me the Eucharist.

We began doing a little prayer service together, before I received Jesus. Then, just as I was about to receive Communion, my little baby let out a few hunger cries. "Can I nurse her while I receive Communion?!" I asked Andrew. "Of course!" he reassured me. So there, resting in my bed and nursing my baby girl, I received the Eucharist for the first time as a brand new mother.

And suddenly, the Eucharist made sense.

My labor and delivery with my first baby were incredibly hard and long. I was in labor for about a day and a half, and by the time I gave birth, I was spent. I had had a very difficult pregnancy, too, suffering from hyperemesis gravidarum (persistent and often severe nausea) for the duration. Then, after giving birth, I was surprised by how often such a little person would want to drink my milk—and by how much I would want to feed her. I had given everything that I had, so that this little child could live. I had nourished her with my very body.

This is my Body, given up for you.

It made sense. It all made sense. I had long prayed that Jesus would give me the grace to love as he loved. Through my vocation as a mother, he had enabled me to do just that. I had given up my very body for the sake of another. I began to cry tears of joy. My prayers had been answered.

In the years since then, I continue to find myself sustained by the Eucharist, and grateful for this precious gift that

Jesus left us. We have a saying in our family, "When life seems overwhelming, take it to Jesus in the Eucharist." My time with Jesus in the Eucharist has fed and strengthened me as a mother, making it possible to totally give of myself.

I'm often struck by the story of the Last Supper and the realization that the Apostles didn't quite comprehend what was happening. They couldn't make the connection between the Eucharistic sacrifice, and the suffering and death of Christ on the cross. They couldn't fully grasp what it meant, for Jesus to give them the gift of his Body and Blood. Yet, Jesus gave totally of himself, even *before* they understood that he was doing so. And even now. . . do we really fully grasp and appreciate what Jesus has left us in the Eucharist? Do we even come close to being able to wrap our minds around a God who is so great, whose love is so immense, and yet who is present to us in a tiny host?

As a mother, it sometimes feels like I am giving, giving, giving. And sometimes, it feels like the more I give, the less I am appreciated. Often, when I do something right, my only thanks is a tantrum. In my less-than-holy moments, I tend to feel frustrated by that. Where is my thanks? Can't they see all that I am doing for them?

And yet, what I am doing for my little ones, the love and care that I am showing them—it is only the smallest taste of the love of Christ for us. Am I as appreciative as I should be, in the face of that great love? Am I as humble as he is, in my own gift of self?

Mary, Mother of the Eucharist, pray for us.

The Sorrowful Mysteries

In the Sorrowful Mysteries, we meet Mary as a sorrowing mother. Motherhood is filled with moments of grief – watching a child suffer or fall away from the faith, suffering yourself from infertility or illness, and so many other sorrows both great and small. Mary is one we can come to in those moments, for she knows the depths of true sorrow, as well as the goodness that God can bring forth from it.

The First Sorrowful Mystery
The Agony in the Garden
Amy Garro

If I am unequal to a mothering trial at hand, I can spend that time asking for God's help—even daring to ask for His help in the form of an angel.

My second born son had a period of time where he was the happiest baby I've ever seen. Complete strangers even commented that they had never seen such a happy child. After he turned one, however, his happy moods slowly subsided and were replaced by crankiness, then misery, and then absolute pain accompanied by hour(s)-long screaming sessions.

As parents, we didn't know what was going on. We didn't know the cause, we didn't know the cure, and we certainly couldn't find any suitable distraction. Once he started crying and screaming, there was nothing to do but hold him and pray that it ended soon. These incidents continued to escalate, and were often the worst at Mass. My husband and I took turns holding him in the narthex. I cried as I watched him turn red, yelling in pain, scratching and injuring his own face and mine in anger and frustration. I didn't know how to help, and didn't know how to cope mentally with his breakdowns.

After months of these episodes, it became unbearable for me as his mother. There was little to nothing I could do, except to be there for him as he suffered. Unfortunately, it was breaking my heart too much. I started calling my husband home from work on the bad days. I had to hand him off and lock myself in our room, the bathroom, *anywhere* else. I wasn't even strong enough to help my own child—his troubles were too burdensome for me to handle. I felt much like the weak disciples, who fell asleep while Christ suffered his agony in the garden. One hour. That's all the longer they usually lasted, and like the disciples, I couldn't do it. I pictured Christ turning to me and questioning me—*You couldn't be with your son for even one hour?* I didn't even have to do anything—just keep watch, like the disciples. Yet I, too, was unable.

Gradually, we started finding answers for our little guy, both from doctors and other mothers, and through trial and error. The screaming was still there, but it lessened over the months. The hard times were fewer and farther in between, making them more manageable. And yet, I still felt like a failure, having deserted my child when he needed me most.

A reading of another gospel account, however, gives a fuller picture. (See Luke 22:39–46.) St. Luke describes the Apostles as having fallen asleep because of their "grief." Luke also describes how Jesus, in His grief, was ministered to by an angel. I found this so comforting. Like the disciples, I was weak—but like the Apostles, it was *due to grief,* not because I lacked faith or love. My inability to stay by my child all through every single screaming session did not mean that I didn't love him—but that I am mortal and get tired. I cannot be everything, at every moment, to my child. As a human, I will never be *everything*. Even Jesus, in his agony, was visited by an angel.

So when I am weak, what am I to do?

If I am unequal to a mothering trial at hand, I can spend that time asking for God's help—even daring to ask for His help in the form of an angel. Through prayer, I must seek for His will to be done—but can ask that if He is willing, He might take the cup away from my child.

As Catholics, we believe that we all have angels watching over us. We can pray to these angels, or ask God to send help through His angels. We can ask our guardian angels to be with us, to strengthen us as they did Christ.

But it doesn't end there—we can ask angels to help *others*. As a mother, there is so much power in praying to your child's guardian angel. Our young ones do not have the words to always pray on their own, and so we pray on their behalf. This mystery of the Rosary taught me that just as God comforted His own son with an angel, He could comfort my son with an angel—and perhaps in deeper ways than I am able to comfort him.

Mary, Queen of the Angels, pray for us.

The Second Sorrowful Mystery
The Scourging at the Pillar
Morgan Caudle

I closed my eyes and begged Our Lady of Sorrows to help me in the way that only a fellow mother, who has been through the pain of watching a child suffer, could.

I've always loved Mary. I loved looking at images of Mary and picturing myself as a mother; however, I preferred happy pictures of Mary with a sweet baby Jesus bouncing on her lap. After all, that is what my life was going to be full of—little children cuddling happily on my lap. When my first two children were born, I would always pray the Joyful and Glorious Mysteries while picturing a smiling Mary with an even more joyful and glorious Son. It was so easy to relate to those mysteries while rocking my beautiful boys to sleep. I never could relate to the Sorrowful Mysteries, especially ones that involved Mary seeing her Son in agony.

That changed in the blink of an eye with the birth of my third and now also my fourth son. Both of my younger children have metabolic disorders that have caused them extreme pain and much suffering.

There were many days that I had to leave the house because I could not take the screaming anymore. One night in particular I was holding a rigid and screaming baby that could only be fed by a tube and I was at the verge of despair. I closed my eyes and begged Our Lady of Sorrows to help me in the way that only a fellow mother, who has been through the pain of watching a child suffer, could. My heart was breaking; my child was suffering greatly through no fault of his own. I was supposed to be able to comfort and protect him but the only thing I could do was watch him scream and writhe in pain. I felt I was failing as a mother.

Up until that night I had avoided Our Lady of Sorrows; she and I had nothing in common (or at least I wanted to have nothing in common with her). However from that night forward during my nightly vigils with my son, I began to meditate on Our Lady's Sorrows. She, too, knew the pain of watching a child in agony. She watched her Son being tortured, knowing full well that He could have stopped it in an instant.

I often pictured her watching Jesus being scourged at the pillar wanting with all of her motherly heart to go and hug her Son. She must have yearned to take that pain from her child just like I wish I could take my children's pain away. However, she also had to know that the pain that Jesus had taken upon Himself was leading to a greater good. The redemption of man was underway; the pain of all sin was being taken upon her Son's innocent shoulders.

In a similar way, when my children are screaming out my name in pain as they lay on a hospital bed being poked and prodded, I want so badly to take their pain away, but I know that their pain is leading to a greater good. I know that soon the poking will be done and they will feel better. Their pain leads to something better, just like Jesus' pain led to something better.

Meditating on Our Lady's view of the Scourging at the Pillar, while witnessing my children's suffering, has reminded me of a great truth: pain can be redemptive. Most often the things that make us holier or better mothers are the things that hurt us the most. I've learned that my job is not to try to take all of the pain out of the lives of my children or myself, but to allow that pain to lead to holiness and a greater good.

I have tried, all my life, to avoid the pain represented in the Sorrowful Mysteries—but now, I am living those mysteries. Yet, God has also given me the grace to see that suffering as a part of the work of salvation.

Mary, Our Lady of Sorrows, pray for us.

The Third Sorrowful Mystery
The Crowning with Thorns
Christy Isinger

We can take comfort in the knowledge that Mary has gone
before us on this path of humiliation.

Whenever I pray the mystery of the Crowning with Thorns I'm

forced to ponder the unthinkable. I'm forced to imagine and

meditate on the torture and humiliation of Christ; the Christ

whom I love and who loves me enough to die for my very

pathetic sins. I want my love for Christ to be as strong as the

love I have for my children. To be honest I don't think I've

reached that point yet, but I've come to know through the love of

my children how sacrificial, boundless, and intense Christ's love

is for me and for us all. This immense and indescribable love is

why Jesus endures the torture of this crowning with thorns. Yet, alongside this physical pain is also the palpable humiliation of Christ, God made man, as he suffers at the hands of his captors. But his love endures even humiliation.

When I meditate upon this mystery I always wonder if there were crowds watching. Did this happen behind closed doors? Were people jeering in cooperation with the soldiers who carried out this deed? Was Mary within view, or did she simply feel the sword pierce her heart at the same moment?

Now, as a mother, I cannot pray the mysteries of the rosary without being called back to what Mary experienced, especially through the sorrowful mysteries. Her journey is parallel to that of Christ's and she remains our perfect example of love and what motherhood really means. In this journey through the suffering of Christ, I am always blown away and full of awe by Mary our mother.

The physical pain of being crowned with a twisted ring of thorns is almost impossible to comprehend. What a horrid example of the capacity for pure evil, pettiness, malice, and violence. We are given the opportunity to journey alongside Mary and Jesus, as we pray this mystery.

Of course, as mothers we understand the depth of anguish a mother experiences when her child is in pain. We know the powerlessness of watching our child suffer. Even the little things—the fevers or the scrapes and bruises—we feel as if they were our own pain. How much more painful must it have been for Mary to watch her Son endure this torture?

What I don't think about as often as I pray these mysteries is what humiliation means, or more importantly, what it might mean for my child to experience humiliation. My children are still very young. I still see them as perfectly formed, innocent people with infinite possibilities and potential. Each word and each glimmer of their burgeoning personalities fills me with a wonder and hope for their future. I am a mother; I see only beautiful potential. I still can't understand or even imagine how difficult it will be to walk with my children in humiliation. I want to do anything and everything I can to shield them from the destructiveness and maliciousness that our world seems full of. I want to protect them from the put-downs, the negatives, the diminishing of what so much of our society is consumed. I want the world to see and appreciate their unique importance, their indescribable dignity, and the gifts that they offer.

How much more then, did Mary feel as her Son—God made man, the Savior of the world—was mocked and humiliated with a crown of vicious, painful thorns? The virtue of the mystery of the crowning with thorns is moral courage. I often ponder this virtue, how it relates to Christ's bravery and perseverance, but more so in regards to Mary's courage. She could have shrank from this unspeakable horror, she could have fallen apart crippled by emotion, or she could have turned her eyes from her precious child's pain. She felt all the indignity, all the offense, all the malicious intent that the wretched crown meant. Yet she remained courageous, even in the face of how much pain she must have felt. Through each horrible injury to her son, each insult, she continued climbing the hill alongside Jesus as he carried the cross. Her moral courage remained with her until the very end, and the end at Golgotha was bitter.

Can I walk alongside my children as they carry their crosses? Can I remain with them even in the face of humiliation? I can easily imagine myself acting badly in the event of my child suffering humiliation. I wouldn't think twice before jumping in to defend them, to knock the offender down a couple pegs, or to set the record straight. But there are many situations where I will be simply unable to do anything. I will most likely face many instances where I will need the moral courage to journey with my child through such pain. I may have to teach or guide, but most likely I will have to pray and hope and pray some more. I will need moral courage to persevere in believing that my prayers will make an impact, that they will indeed help my child, that the pain of humiliation they may feel will be healed by Him who suffered humiliation as well. I know this quiet discipline of moral courage isn't as dramatic as the martyr who stands in direct opposition to the dictator, knowing the firing squad awaits, yet there exists so much temptation to doubt, that the effort feels heroic.

But Mary's journey conquered the same doubts I struggle with. Mary journeyed with her Son through the unthinkable. She experienced every anguish imaginable as her Son was tortured and killed. Mary's prayers and presence endured even a cruel crowning of thorns. We can take comfort in the knowledge that Mary has gone before us on this path of humiliation. Young mothers like me need to know that we will have courage when the day comes, to be with our children through their own humiliation.

Mary, Humble of Heart, pray for us.

The Fourth Sorrowful Mystery
Jesus Carries His Cross
Kate Mattoon

Again, like so many times before, I prayed desperately for the wisdom to know how to help her carry her cross, and for the strength to not be crushed by the weight of it.

"¿Ya terminaron?" Are you finished?

The stern voice reached us through the low hanging branches of the mango trees.

"!No, Tía!" "!Ya voy, Tía!" "¡Casi termino Tía!" The little girls yelled, almost in unison, as they scattered from their seats on and around a broken wooden bench where we had been seated together, eating sticky mangos that had fallen to the ground all around us. They grabbed their rakes and pails and hurriedly continued the work of cleaning the miniature mango

111

grove that made up most of their front yard. I watched them work, the sweat dripping down their dirty faces, which they wiped occasionally on their ragged play-clothes, and marveled at their discipline and focus on the task at hand.

As I watched them, I let my mind wander back to our conversation just moments before. Seeing that their caretaker, their Tía, was on the phone, one by one the girls had left their work behind, grabbed a mango off the ground, and flopped down on to the strangely tilted bench under the biggest, shadiest tree, or straight onto the ground, to eat. My goddaughter Brittany had wandered over with two mangos, one of which she had valiantly attempted to clean on her tattered, dirt-caked shirt before handing to me. "My godparents never visit me, and they never give me gifts," Kimberly had complained as she joined us on the bench. "My godmother just tells me, 'My gift is my LOOOOVE,'" she had said, with all the pre-adolescent attitude she could muster. "Ugghhhh."

"I know what a godmother is," Brittany said, seeming to have ignored her older sister's commentary. "A godmother is your third mother! First you have the Virgin Mary, then your mom, then your godmother."

"But you don't HAVE a mom," Cati, the youngest of the girls living in the home, had said, blunt as always. "That makes Kate your second mother, just behind Mary."

"I am going to ask for a soccer jersey for my birthday," continued Kimberly, as if Brittany and Cati had never chimed in, "One from the Honduran national team."

The girls had then chattered about the upcoming birthday celebration for all of the kids who had a cumpleaños in the month of June, and I had let their words swirl around me with the mosquitos and wasps, focusing my attention on my goddaughter's tiny body next to me. At the age of nine, she still wore clothes made for a toddler, though what she lacked in size she made up for in personality. Her second mother. . . just behind the Virgin Mary? Had I known what becoming her godmother would really mean when she asked me nearly three years ago, would I have said yes?

A wasp landed on my leg, where one of the little girls must have touched me with sticky mango hands. I brushed it away and walked over to the nearby water spout to wash myself off. I saw a discarded rake on the ground, and remembered how, an hour prior, I had walked all around the orphanage property with Brittany, trying to find an extra rake or two to borrow to help the yard work go more quickly. Of course, the only house with extra rakes was the oldest boys' house, the furthest house from the little girls', and the very last place we stopped to look. On the walk back with the rakes, Brittany had stopped in front of the youngest boys' house. I stopped beside her, and she looked up at me. Though barely three feet tall, the look on her face was anything but the look of a child. "My brothers are gone." She had said quietly.

"Yo sé." I answered. I know. "Lo siento mucho." I am so sorry.

"It's just me and my sisters now."

"You are lucky to have them." I told her, but my words sounded all wrong when I said them out loud. "I pray for you and your siblings every day."

She didn't answer, and I didn't try to say anything else. There was nothing else to say. I felt like my heart had fallen all the way down the bottom of the hole the little boys were digging to bury their own rotting mangos. A year ago Brando, the younger of Brittany's two older brothers would have been right with the other boys, digging and hauling away dirt like a little man. And Duncan, the older of the two, would have been nearby as well, probably throwing rotting mangos at the other boys as they tried to get their chores done.

But living in a country whose social structure has been torn apart by drugs, poverty, and violence, Duncan and Brando came to the orphanage too broken to be put together by a place with such limited resources. Unable to conform to the structure of life in their new home, first Duncan, then Brando were separated from their only remaining family—their siblings—to live in secure government facilities until their eighteenth birthdays. At ages eleven and thirteen, they still had a long way to go.

Brittany had turned away from the boys, and kept walking. I followed her. She dragged her rake behind her now, and stared somewhat blankly at the dirt path ahead of her. And again, like so many times before, I prayed desperately for the wisdom to know how to help her carry her cross, and for the strength to not be crushed by the weight of it; to somehow, be as strong as her:

Mother Mary, I do not know how you could stand to watch your son carrying his cross to Calvary. I don't know how you did it, and I don't know how to stand by and watch my tiny goddaughter carry the heaviest of crosses. I don't know how to care for her when I have so little control over what happens to her and the people she loves. I don't know how to keep her safe as she grows up in the most violent country in the world. I feel broken by the weight of watching her suffer, of feeling helpless to ease her burden or her pain. But I know you love Brittany, and trust you to step in and be her mother in all of the ways in which I fall short. Please comfort her in times of sorrow and pray for her in her moments of need. And please pray for me, that I may have the wisdom and strength to do what you did on the first Good Friday; to stand up to an unjust, broken world by being present to those who suffer, no matter how overwhelmed I feel by the pain I see.

Then suddenly, the little girls had surrounded me again.

"!Ya terminamos, ya terminamos!" they told me. "Will you take us to the park?" The front yard was spotless; even the wasps seemed to have realized that there was nothing sweet for them to enjoy here, and had moved on. I agreed to take them and they ran to their Tía, asking permission to go with me. Brittany ran back to me and grabbed my hand. "¡Vamos!" she yelled. "¡Corre!" Let's go! Run! Their excitement was contagious and I was swept away running with them. They raced all the way to the swings, jumped on, and started to yell-sing what, for some reason, had always been their favorite swinging song:

Vienen con alegría Señor, cantando
Vienen con alegría Señor
Los que caminan por la vida Señor, sembrando tu paz y amor.

They come with happiness, Lord, singing
They come with happiness, Lord
They who walk for life, Lord, planting your peace and Love.

Mary, Comfort of the Afflicted, pray for us.

The Fifth Sorrowful Mystery
The Crucifixion
Katie Schulte

I feel so blessed to have Mary as our heavenly mother—one who also truly and fully understands the devastating loss of a child.

The Crucifixion—the brutal, agonizing death of Jesus on the cross—can be a difficult mystery to contemplate and identify with. Yes, we've all had serious, painful losses in our lives. But can we really compare them to Mary watching Jesus be crucified? I have struggled with this question, and have actually come to think that *not* comparing misses the point. We are all called to imitate Christ by taking up our own crosses and uniting them with His. As mothers, we are *also* called to imitate Mary by faithfully "standing at the foot" of the crosses of our children. But what does that *mean*? To answer a difficult question with a simple answer: I believe it begins with the understanding that our children are not really our own. Mary fully grasped and lived this truth.

It must have been difficult for her to watch Jesus begin His public ministry, all the while knowing that in some way a "sword would pierce her heart" (Luke 2:35). There must have been part of her that just wanted to hold Him in her arms and not let Him leave the safety of their quiet home. But, in faithful obedience to God, Mary supported Jesus and helped Him fulfill God's plan for His life, even when it was difficult or painful for her to do so. In fact, she even initiated His first miracle at the wedding feast in Cana, as if she were giving Him her blessing.

Despite our most faithful attempts, nothing is more challenging than giving our children back to God—entrusting them to His providence and care. And as a young mother, I'm learning that this surrendering is an ongoing process for me. There are days when it is easy to entrust my children to God, and there are days when it is the last thing I want to do. But in the end, I know that all I have and am comes from God. And although God gives me the gift of caring for my children in this lifetime, in the end, they, too, belong only to Him.

I thought I knew what it meant to be vulnerable, and then my son John was born, and it took me to an entirely new level of vulnerability. It was as though John was my heart, which was now physically removed from my body and exposed to the world: to be hurt, to be taken. Though my heart was bursting with love and gratitude for having him in my life, I was afraid that I would always be gripped with fear.

John is my second child. My first baby, whom we named Teresa, was lost to miscarriage. So, the idea of losing John before he was born haunted me. My mother would wisely say, "You just have to trust God, honey." And although I knew her advice was true, I argued back silently that I *had* trusted God before. . . and my baby died. It happened to me once; why not twice? To me, the loss of a child was no longer an abstract and tragic thought, but my real and painful lived experience. It was hard to offer my son to God and trust when it felt as though that trust had been broken. I wasn't exactly mad at God, because I believe that God does not *cause* bad things to happen to us, but rather the bad things that happen are the natural consequence of living in a fallen world. But even given my intellectual understanding about the nature of evil, *I felt forsaken.*

The loss I endured was too tangible and intense for me to be comforted by philosophical explanations. In fact, I now find comfort believing that sometimes suffering is too complicated for human comprehension; that when it comes to losing our children or seeing them in pain, only our all-knowing God can ever truly understand and explain it. And somehow that brings me peace.

Since losing Teresa, I find it very consoling to talk with others who have lived through the same experience and truly understand my loss. That's why I feel so blessed to have Mary as our heavenly mother—one who also *truly and fully* understands the devastating loss of a child. Mary, most blessed and favored of all God's creatures, was not spared this loss, and there is great solace in knowing she shares this journey with us—with me. She, too, felt the incredible agony and emptiness that comes from the death of one's child. She, too, understands the torment of watching her son suffering and in pain. And though she did not experience it personally, I'm sure her heart aches with compassion when she sees us loving our children even when they turn away from God and make bad decisions.

Our first child, Teresa, was due on October 15, the feast of St. Teresa of Avila. My husband and I try to do something special that day to celebrate her life. Every year, I think I am the one remembering her. . . but more often than not, I feel her reaching out to me. On what would have been her first birthday, I was thinking about her when I received a text from my husband's aunt. She invited me to a Mass that night being offered for all families grieving the loss of a baby. She had no idea that it was the anniversary of Teresa's due date. I felt so strongly this was a sign from my child letting me know she was still with me, an enduring presence in my life.

On what would have been Teresa's third birthday, my doctor scheduled an ultrasound (I didn't request this date) and we learned we were welcoming a baby girl, our third child. As I sat down to unwind that evening, still beaming with our joyful news, I discovered that October 15 is *Infant and Pregnancy Loss Awareness Day.* Apparently, it was instituted in 2006 by the House of Representatives as a Day of Remembrance. Who knew? Again, I felt that my daughter was blowing me a kiss from heaven, telling me she was celebrating with our family that day.

I don't share these stories to give the impression that I always see things with heaven in sight; I'm afraid that's just not true. But in my dark moments, I rely on these experiences for consolation and hope. They are a reminder to me that, in the whole big picture which only God understands, Teresa is as much a part of our family from heaven as she was on earth. Even though I would still prefer to have seen Teresa's face and held her in my arms, I do believe we have an irreplaceable mother and child bond. It is my hope that when I leave this life, she will be holding my hand and welcoming me into the next.

Perhaps Mary had similar thoughts running through her head in those three days after Jesus' death. Maybe, after watching Jesus be killed, she wondered just how God was going to keep His promise that her Son would rule over the house of Jacob forever and of His kingdom there would "be no end" (Luke 1:33)? Whether such thoughts crossed her mind or not, we know Mary's faithfulness was unwavering. Her complete trust and reliance on God tells us that, although she may have wondered about His plan, she never doubted Him and His love for her.

Mary, Virgin Most Faithful, pray for us.

The Glorious Mysteries

In the Glorious Mysteries, Mary shows us the final end of our motherhood. She reminds us that God has made us for heaven, and that by her Son's cross and resurrection, the gates of heaven have been opened to us. She is the first to taste the glory of Christ, who is resurrected from the dead, and now reigns in heaven. She shows us the glory that is to come, and reminds us to keep running the race.

The First Glorious Mystery
The Resurrection
Dwija Borobia

*God loves us as much as he loved those women rushing to his
tomb on the third day. . . He wants us to run to him in our
heartbroken and miserable moments so that he can give us new
eyes to see and new hearts to love.*

It is a rare night, even without a newborn in the house, that I
sleep for more than six hours straight. Those glorious,
wonderful, beautiful nuggets of sanity are tucked like shining
beacons into the tiny spaces between wide expanses of multiple
wake-ups by children of various ages; people climbing into and
out of our bed; complaints of bad dreams, itchy elbows, or the
very real fear of jam being stuck in someone's eye. . . despite the
complete lack of food anywhere in the vicinity (my response to
this was probably less than admirable, but thankfully I've

succeeded in blocking most of the ridiculous exchange from my mind).

And it is a rare day that I go more than an hour without some child doing something I might call frustrating, saying something I might call unreasonable, being something that I might call difficult. There are fights and messes and, on some days, a seemingly endless barrage of complaints that become requests that become demands.

Under difficult circumstances—when your child is ill, struggling, or fighting a battle no one on earth can help him win—parenting can surely feel like we are getting a small foretaste of death. But it seems to me that things don't have to be going poorly for this to be true. It seems to me that even under the most ideal conditions, motherhood can sometimes feel like we're being asked to die a thousand little deaths every single day.

In the big picture we experience the death of our schedule, the death of our sleep, the death of our ability to leave our crafting supplies out on the table while we make dinner. In the details we find the death of our vision of perfect behavior at This Extremely Important Event, the death of the peaceful afternoon we were imagining right before someone smeared yogurt on the baby, the deaths of every breakable item resting four or fewer feet above the floor. And this is when things are going well! Yes, even when things are normal and regular and good, this fallen world is sure to leave us feeling the sting of death.

Since my conversion fourteen years ago, I've kept the notion of Jesus conquering death tucked safely in the Big Picture section in the back of my mind. The problem with this is twofold. First of all, this crucial victory is not just a notion, some far away idea. No, this victory is the ultimate reality of the

Christian. It is the very foundation of our faith and the thing we are blessed to be able to live day in and day out.

Secondly, and perhaps even more importantly, our God is not just a Big Picture God. Certainly He is waiting for us at the end of this journey, this adventure, and he can see everything at every moment. There is no doubt there. But our God is with us in all the little details, too. Our God is an Every Little Moment God.

When the women went to the tomb, they were heartbroken and miserable. The worst thing that could possibly happen had happened. Yet even that worst thing, that final, terrible thing, was no match for God. He took that loss and he turned it into a victory. A victory for all time and all people, undoubtedly, but also a victory for that time and the real, individual people standing there. When Jesus died, his friends experienced a death too. They suffered the death of the life they had known, the death of their dreams and expectations, the death of what they thought would surely happen in the world. And when Jesus came back to life, he gave them a new life too! Not just a someday new life after the resurrection of their bodies, but a new life right then—new dreams, new hopes, brand new eyes and hearts with which to see and love the world.

Then one day, not too long ago, it dawned on me. God loves us as much as he loved those women rushing to his tomb on the third day. He wants to do for us exactly what he did for them. He wants us to run to him in our heartbroken and miserable moments so that he can give us new eyes to see and new hearts to love.

He is with me in the long shuffle down the hall at 2 a.m. with a toddler, mumbling unintelligibly, draped across my arms. He is with me when I don't think I can make it another week or day or even hour with the constant demands that are being made on my body, mind, and spirit alike. He is with me in the wiping and the scrubbing, the soothing and the encouraging, the smiles and the tears. He is with me in the good-mommy moments and the moments I hope my children will, in their kindness, wipe from their memories.

When Jesus defeated death, he didn't just defeat Death, the loss of life in its biggest, most final form. If that were the case we'd have to wait our entire lives to accept and enjoy what he so selflessly suffered to give us. But because he is not just a Big Picture God, an End of the Road God, our Every Little Moment God didn't just conquer one death. He conquered every death. He conquered the big Death *and all the little deaths*. If we cling to our Lord, every tiny death we die as parents has a new life waiting for us on the other side. A new life and a better self, with fresh eyes to see our children as He sees us, and new hearts to love the world the way He calls us to love.

Mary, Morning Star, pray for us.

The Second Glorious Mystery
The Ascension
Jenna Hines

*I needed to redefine my end game. The end is not self-reliance.
The end is total reliance on Him.*

The thought of running a marathon now is laughable to me. But, back before I had three kids, when I was unmarried, when I didn't have a career just yet, I figured there wasn't much else to do. I jogged (or rather shuffled) along through the training program, never having done more than an 8K in my life. And I was feeling pretty proud of myself on the days when I could churn out ten or more miles.

It was one of those days that I attempted to run fifteen miles in the muggy drizzle of a summer morning. Somewhere around that fifteenth mile, I began to feel weak. In retrospect, it was dehydration and exhaustion, but in the moment, I thought I had met my end. Perhaps that sounds embellished, but what turned out to be a panic attack had me believing nothing less than the worst.

That weekend run was my first experience with panic disorder, and I would have many episodes following it. I still do. Looking back now, it was clear; however, it took me months to finally figure out that the problem came from the hardwiring in my head.

A pounding heart, night terrors, shortness of breath, dizziness, feelings of being out of control. These are just some of the many symptoms I felt overwhelmed by on almost a daily basis. I no longer felt safe driving, exercising, or even going out alone. My life was being taken away from me by a complete mystery.

The first thing I turned to after considerable hesitation was medication. I needed to get help fast so I could spend my energy figuring out how to manage. Various prescriptions were written up for me, and I was finally able to feel like I had a bit of control over what I was slowly learning to be panic attacks.

The next step was therapy. I sought out a Catholic therapist who might cure my problems. Weeks into the program, I felt that I had more control, but I was disappointed to learn that my panic attacks might never go away. There was no cure; there was only management.

Supplements, diets, more medication, oils, rubs, this, that and the other thing. Everything was given a fair shake. All I wanted was to feel the control I once had. I didn't want to live day-to-day wondering about the next attack. I wanted to know that my mind was my own, and I had complete sovereignty over it.

Feelings of panic and lack of control only got worse as hormones surged through my body each and every pregnancy. It often seems like a cruel joke that we are called to withstand the discomfort of pregnancy, birth and the postpartum period all on raging hormones and little sleep. And these little souls that I have been entrusted with made me yearn for that perfect mental clarity even more so.

I "knew" that if I could just pull myself together somehow, I would be able to be the perfect mother for them. I "knew" that with this cross of anxiety, I would never be able to fully trust myself with their care. Certainly, other moms did not share my worry that I wouldn't be able to take care of them when it really mattered.

The attacks still bombarded my life whenever they felt like it, and I was beginning to wear down. After one particularly frightening episode, my family stepped in more than they ever had before. My mother called a local priest who was known to perform miracles. He agreed to see me and assess my situation.

Father prayed over me and asked questions to gain an understanding of my situation. He assured me that the visions and gifts he has are not of his own accord. Everything he had been given had been gifted by the Lord; Father was merely the instrument. He put me on a steady and powerful regimen of various types of prayer. And, while I did not receive an immediate miracle in that visit, I learned a priceless lesson.

I had spent an incredible amount of time focusing on how to do this on my own. I wanted control of my mind. I wanted to find the miracle cure. I wanted to defeat this. And I didn't know how I was expected to do it on my own. Frankly, when the idea of prayer even entered my mind, I thought that I would be able to pray about it, be healed, and forget the entire thing. I was looking forward to a time when I wouldn't need to rely on remedies or even God anymore—when I would only need myself.

I needed to redefine my end game. The end is not self-reliance. The end is total reliance on Him. We will spend the rest of our lives on this imperfect planet amid sorrow and tragedy, pain and suffering. There is no end to our need for Christ. But, as He promised, if we remain faithful we will one day be with Him in the Glorious Kingdom, enjoying the goods of Heaven.

Not only do we believe that Christ ascended into the kingdom that has no end, we also believe that He left us the comfort of His mother, and this has been incredibly important to me while I wade through anxious times. Not only is Jesus the King of Heaven, but His mother is queen—a powerful intercessor who no doubt understands the demands and trials of motherhood. We have been given the ability to call upon her, and she will speak to her Son about our troubles. Who better to pray for me while I nurture children and an anxiety disorder?

Our Mother Mary had everything to be anxious about. She watched her Son ascend the throne as King of Heaven. And, while she may have known that He was destined for greatness from the moment He was conceived, did that make it any easier to watch Him die, rise and then be taken away from her again forty days later to a paradise unknown?

What must she have been thinking as she watched her Son leave her one last time? Did she know that He would be the final answer to all of our worldly suffering? While we may not know for sure, we do know that Mary possessed lively faith, blind obedience, heroic patience and divine wisdom. She certainly would have trusted that her Son was up to something prodigious, and she would have endured any emotional suffering with grand conviction.

From Mary's example, I know the Lord does not wish suffering upon me, but He will use my cross for a greater good. And I do not stop searching for relief from my panic attacks because I know God will not leave me to suffer unaided. But, things will happen in His perfect time—which is not necessarily my own timeline. So as I continue to seek comfort (and probably will for years to come), I keep my mind on the idea that independence is not the goal. Total reliance on the Ascended King is the closest I will come to perfection until I am able to join Him in His kingdom.

Mary, Mother Most Admirable, pray for us.

The Third Glorious Mystery
Pentecost
Michele E. Chronister

More than anything else, though, I think that Mary is a peaceful presence in a chaotic world.

I will never forget the night that we brought our firstborn home from the hospital. Prior to giving birth to Therese, neither of us had any experience taking care of babies. On the maternity floor, I'd gained a false sense of confidence. Therese mostly just slept, nursed, and needed diaper changes. She seemed to settle down quickly when I nursed her. Two days in, I felt like a pro.

We brought Therese home from the hospital, and invited her uncles over to meet her. In the course of their visit, she "woke up" a bit (as newborns are wont to do when they are two days old) and began fussing. Her uncles left, and the fussing escalated to crying. Suddenly, I didn't feel so confident. I realized that I *had no idea what I was doing*. Exhausted and hormonal, I turned to Andrew and said, "We have to take her back! We have to take her back to the hospital! We don't know what we're doing. They know what they're doing!" I just wanted to go straight back to my safe and cozy hospital room, with the help of a postpartum nurse only a click of the "help button" away.

Thankfully, Andrew took control of the situation. He sent me to take a shower, and to calm down. When I emerged from the shower, it was quiet. I wandered upstairs and found Andrew laying with Therese on his chest. I heard the gentle clicking of his rosary beads. She was sound asleep. He had prayed her to sleep.

It may have been the first time, but it certainly wasn't the last time that Andrew prayed one of our babies to sleep. In that moment when my anxiety heightens and I try to re-gain control, he tends to relax, relinquish control, and pick up his rosary beads. That tendency has been a blessing in our family.

I often think of just how *scared* the Apostles were in that upper room, on Pentecost. Before the Ascension, I suppose they gained a false sense of confidence. You can sense their increasing joy and eagerness, as the Gospels draw to a close. Then, Jesus ascends back to heaven, and all of a sudden we find them cowering in fear in an upper room.

Yet, Mary was right there with them, Tradition tells us. And she was not afraid.

When the Holy Spirit descended upon them, rushing at them like wind and appearing as tongues of fire, everything changed. Suddenly, they had the grace they needed to do what Jesus called them to do. Suddenly, they had the courage they needed to spread the Gospel.

I wonder what Mary, mother of the Church, was doing in that upper room. Certainly, she wasn't cowering in fear. Was she interceding for them? She, who had already received the Holy Spirit (when He descended upon her at the Annunciation), was already full of grace. Was she, possibly, praying for the Apostles at the very moment that the Holy Spirit rushed in? Did God work through her trusting prayers, as she relied so completely on the promise of her Son?

I *wish* that I could say that I'm just like Mary. In my best moments, I can be somewhat trusting. But overall? I am an anxious person. All too often, I give in to fear.

Almost five years into this parenting gig, I still struggle with bouts of anxiety and fear. Sometimes, in those anxious moments, I recall that image of Andrew, praying over a sleeping Therese. My husband has a special love for the Blessed Mother, and I am so grateful for those times that he has reminded me to turn to her, too. She is a powerful intercessor.

More than anything else, though, I think that Mary is a peaceful presence in a chaotic world. The air in that upper room was thick with fear on Pentecost morning. Yet, in the midst of that atmosphere of fear, we find our Blessed Mother quietly praying. In the midst of so much fear, she was a reminder that there is another way—the way of trust. There is the way of total reliance on the grace of the Holy Spirit, to move within us. Mary knew that whatever she was able to accomplish was not due to any strength on her part. Rather, it was due to the strength of the Holy Spirit at work in her.

This is the reminder that I continue to need as a mother. I have a tendency to try to handle everything myself, rather than ask for help. It is difficult enough for me to ask my husband—who is visibly, physically present on a daily basis—to help me through the rough days. It is even more of a challenge to remember to bring my struggles and frustrations to God.

Yet, this is what Mary challenges me to do. She challenges me to be a presence of peace in my home, trusting the Holy Spirit to work through me. She challenges me to not be in control of everything, but rather, to take things to prayer and trust that God will provide, just as He did on Pentecost.

Mary, Mother Most Amiable, pray for us.

The Fourth Glorious Mystery
The Assumption
Mary Helen Wofford

What we do is no small task. We may not be raising the Son of God, but we are bringing up the next generation of saints.

Despite being one of the principal feast days for the Blessed Virgin Mary, very little is historically known about the Feast of the Assumption. The date, place, and events surrounding it are shrouded in mystery. What we do know is that at the end of her earthly life, our Blessed Mother was assumed body and soul into heaven. The Church has held tight to this tradition since the early Church Fathers, and it was made a dogma of the faith by Pope Pius XII in 1950. While most of the proof for the Assumption comes from Tradition, it is still easy to imagine God's love extending to this event. As mothers, we know the love we have for our children. We also experience the love our children have for us. The bond between mother and child, even in our imperfect homes and families, glues us together. So why would our Savior, whose love for His own Mother is a perfect love, not desire her to reside forever in heaven with him? Why would our Blessed Mother be preserved from Original Sin, but then her earthly body be made to wait for the day we shall all join in the Resurrection? It makes perfect sense that perfect love would bring Mary, body and soul, to heaven.

However, it is not just this perfect love that is depicted in the mystery of the Assumption. Rather, the faithfulness of God is so fully displayed in this Mystery that it makes me wonder why I ever dare to question our Lord's will for my life. At the Annunciation, when Mary became the Mother of God, so began her journey of trust despite suffering. An unplanned pregnancy, the prophecy of Simeon, losing her twelve-year-old child, watching her Son preach and be misunderstood, and finally watching him suffer horrendous torture and death. . . how her heart must have stung throughout her journey of motherhood. And yet, she remained faithful to the Lord because she intimately knew and trusted *His faithfulness.* While I often wonder at Mary's strength to have stood at the bottom of the cross, it is the ascension of her Son—only forty days after his resurrection—that seems more painful to me. To have finally had him back after death, only to see him leave her once again? In my imperfect, human-nature stained heart, it would have been hard for me to not have despaired and been angry. But she stays faithful and waits for the Holy Spirit in the upper room. She trusted in God's promise that He would be with them always. And because of her faithfulness, God rewards her by making her queen over heaven and earth.

The mysteries of the Rosary constantly remind me that God's ways are not always clear. Maybe in the midst of it all, when her Son was dying, when her son was in the tomb, God did not seem present. How often do we feel that way? How often does it feel like God has abandoned us? It can be easy to be swallowed up by feelings of abandonment and despair rather than meditate on how God remains true to His promises. Personally, I struggle with the fact that God's faithfulness in our lives does not always appear instantaneously. But that is why I find this mystery of the Assumption so powerful. It forces me to recognize that God's faithfulness *is* real. He will not abandon us. We may suffer in this life, we may go through low valleys that never seem to end. But, as long as we keep our Lord in our midst, He will always be faithful to us. He will always save us.

When my husband and I got married, we were open to children but wanted to wait a bit to get our family started. God, as He usually does, had other plans. The day I found out I was pregnant with my first I was filled with so many mixed emotions. I was scared, happy, relieved, and anxious all at the same time. We had only been married 6 months; how were we going to do this? We lived in a one bedroom condo; where was baby going to go? We had student loans, and how were we going to pay those off if I wanted to stay home with the baby? How *was* I going to be able to stay home with the baby? And the questions went on and on. As the pregnancy continued, God took care of many of the things that were causing me stress and anxiety. Over time, the fear I had felt melted away to joy and excitement. Our first son was born on a cold January night; and a few days later, we brought home our little baby boy. What followed were the longest 3 weeks of my life.

I still remember the phone call like it was yesterday. When your pediatrician calls to tell you that your baby's liver is failing, you do not forget that. I kept asking him what that meant, not wanting to use the phrase "Is he going to die?" despite so fiercely needing to know the answer. Finally the pediatrician responded with, "Mary Helen, I don't know what this will bring. It is not good, but all you can do tonight is love your baby and pray." As I hung up, I sank to the floor, holding my son, sobbing and screaming for my husband. All I could get out to him was that our baby was dying. This little one, *my* little one, this poor baby who wouldn't gain weight, who seemed in pain all night and slept all day, this poor little one was so sick. I was his mother and could do nothing to help him. That phone call. . . it left a wound in my heart that I have tried desperately to unite with Mary's when Simeon tells her of Jesus' future suffering. And that has brought me strength and consolation.

The next day we took our sweet babe to the children's hospital to determine the cause of his liver failure. After about a week of tests, the cause was narrowed down, and he went into a 6 hour surgery in hopes to buy us more time with his own liver. For those who have ever been in a Children's Hospital Surgery Floor waiting room, you know the faces of parents who have been holding it together for their child. I sat alone for the majority of the surgery just staring into space. I could not let my mind truly think about what was happening. There was so much pain in my heart that I wanted to feel nothing at all. Of course I prayed, but mostly I questioned why all of this had to happen. Why did God want to surprise me with a baby only to take him away from me? Where was God's faithfulness to me now?

When the surgery was over, they brought us into the ICU. His little body was so pale, with wires and tubes all over him. His tiny body, in comparison to the full stretcher he was on, made the enormity of the situation even more poignant. But there was a sense of relief that we were on the right path and that my boy would be ok. We were told he would need to stay about a week to recover, but what we didn't know was that our journey had just begun.

We would spend over a month recovering in the NICU, fighting his inability to tolerate feeds, his failure to thrive, more tests, more pokes, more pricks, more suffering. Finally, we received an answer. Our son was diagnosed with a rare, recessive genetic disorder that left his future and his abilities in the balance. The night before we received this second diagnosis, I had been sitting in the hall of the hospital on the phone with a friend. Ironically, I was telling her that I just did not think I could handle another "thing" going wrong. Therefore, to say I held it together well after this diagnosis would be a horrible lie. Weren't things supposed to be getting better now? Why did God have to keep getting my hopes up only to disappoint me? I felt as if I had lost my child and my future children. Since it was a genetic disorder, it meant that every child we conceived would have a 25% chance of also inheriting this syndrome. My dreams for my family and my baby seemed to end. Would he ever walk or talk? Would he have friends? Play baseball with his dad? Have siblings? Everything I had envisioned for my boy was gone.

They say a diagnosis helps give parents strength because it provides something to fight against, and I suppose that is true.

Once we started to recover from the shock of it all, I began to think a bit more clearly. Despite feeling abandoned by God, I saw how far from the truth that was. God had never been closer to me. He was the one who held me as I left my baby each night in the NICU. He was in every face of every nurse and doctor who so graciously led me through that time. He coached me through each therapy session. And He remained so very faithful to us by surrounding us with countless friends and family who provided emotional and physical support. It was I who had to learn to trust Him despite suffering. And while I know God would had been faithful even if things had not turned out as well as they have, He has blessed us with a very resilient little boy who has beat all the odds. He will always be our miracle, our visible reminder of God's faithfulness in our lives.

I wish I could say that because of all the difficulties with our first child I am a changed woman who knows how to count her blessings and never doubt God's faithfulness. Unfortunately, the minutiae of the day-to-day—the loneliness of staying at home with small children, the constant tantrums and whining, the laundry that never ends—it all often leads me to wonder if God cares about this little life we live. It can be hard to see Jesus in a snot-covered, food-stained face. But the reality is, He's here with us. Always. He promised us His faithfulness as long as we cling to Him. So we must cling to Him, just as Mary clung to her Son. Because just as our Blessed Mother was called from birth to do a special job for the Kingdom of God, we too are doing work for the Kingdom. What we do is no small task. We may not be raising the Son of God, but we are bringing up the next generation of saints. And in turn, I believe they are making us saints as well. God may not reveal Himself in large ways, as in the Annunciation or the Assumption. Sometimes, He may reveal himself in an overwhelming sense of grace and ability to be patient with a wayward child. Sometimes He may show himself in friends and family who have become "your village." It may be in a husband who reminds you that you are still very lovely to him. But with every day that goes by, God continues to provide us with daily miracles to show us He remains present. It is up to us to be attune to that reality, and to look to Mary as our guide. For it is in Mary that we see not only the perfection of Christian life, but also the perfection of God's faithfulness and love. Mary receives what we all long to receive. Let us cling to her that she may show us the way to her Son, even in the dirtiest of times, so that we may rejoice with her in the world to come.

Mary, Virgin Most Faithful, pray for us.

The Fifth Glorious Mystery
The Coronation
Kelly Mantoan

She is a queen, but not one placed on a throne, out of the reach of those who need her.

The beginnings of my Catholic faith started in the front seat of my boyfriend's car, as we were driving to a friend's house, a movie, or wherever, and I was asking questions about this strange religion of his. He was the first and only Catholic I knew at the time. I remember playing with the rosary he kept in his cup holder asking, "What's with these bead things?" And "What's the big deal about Mary?" He hardly took his eyes off the road to say, "Well, she was chosen to be the MOTHER OF GOD, so that kind of makes her important."

Indeed, it did seem obvious. Why was the one woman who—out of all of the women throughout history—was chosen to carry the Word made Flesh, just given a token mention during my Methodist Christmas service? I had to agree. Mary was important, and when I reread the stories around the life of Christ, Mary was there through so much more besides just the Nativity.

As I waded deeper into my future husband's faith I realized that the Church taught more about Mary than what was in the Bible. Tradition had a lot to offer. Before I joined the Church in 2001, tradition meant dressing up every Sunday and sitting in the same pew. I remember studying an illustrated rosary pamphlet and realizing that it was more than just some beads. I recognized many of the mysteries from my days in Sunday School until I came to the end of the Glorious Mysteries—the Assumption of Mary followed by her Coronation as Queen of Heaven and Earth. I could follow the Church's logic behind Mary's assumption. But crowning her Queen? It seemed like wishful thinking and I couldn't understand what the point of it was. I knew Mary was worthy of my admiration, but putting her in heaven as a Queen, next to Christ our King, who was a Person of the triune God? Well, didn't that just smack of "Catholics worshipping Mary"?

I had a lot more to learn about Mary. My newborn faith was too shallow. There was a lot I didn't know and hadn't thought to ask during my conversion process. There was more to her than the beautiful statues topped with a floral wreath. She wore an eternal crown for a reason, and I knew I had to find out why.

I questioned my husband, and he answered the best he could, and pointed me towards Revelation, where a woman is described who is "clothed with the sun" who has a "crown of twelve stars." (See Revelation 12:1.)

These allusions to Mary were a lot harder for me to understand, but once I started looking I realized they were more numerous than I realized. Despite my lack of understanding, I never shied away from Mary. Within a year of my conversion, I was married and pregnant with our first child. I had jumped in the deep end of the Catholic pool and was quickly in over my head. I said the rosary as often as I could, using that worn rosary pamphlet to help me learn the prayers and mysteries.

I had our oldest daughter, then son, we moved, got pregnant again, moved again. Mary was always there, even when I was overwhelmed, exhausted and unable to make time to pray. For many years I just moved blindly through my faith, unable to find the time to learn more. But then shortly after the birth of my third, I started praying the Little Office of the Blessed Virgin Mary, which led me to the Old Testament where many passages also talked about a woman who could only be Mary. How could I have not seen the significance of these passages before? Mary was everywhere! Most memorably, I remember the passage from Genesis where a woman is described who will "crush the head" of the serpent.

I started reading more about the history and traditions of the Church and learned Mary was officially declared the Mother of God, or Theotokos, at the First Council of Ephesus all the way back in 431.

It seemed more and more outrageous to me to not regard Mary as a Queen. As with all the teachings of the Church, the Coronation of Mary, which seemed foreign to me as a convert, were backed up by scripture and a thousand years of tradition.

The more I understood Mary's importance, the closer I came to her. A casual acquaintance started by faith, become a strong devotion based on unwavering confidence. The mystery that seemed the farthest from acceptance soon came to signify a great bond between Our Lady and our family.

Because Mary is in heaven, and revered so by even her Son, I can have confidence in her intercession, whether I invoke her as Queen of Heaven and Earth or any of her other numerous titles. Seated in heaven, near our Lord, I can picture her leaning in and speaking in His ear my worries, fears, and disappointments. What loving son can refuse his mother?

Now, in times of sorrow and joy, I turn without hesitation to Mary. When I was overwhelmed with grief after each of my two youngest sons were diagnosed with a degenerative neuromuscular disease, Mary comforted me, and when I was too angry with God to pray, I still asked for her help. When I had to leave one of my boys in a hospital room, I trusted her to keep watch. I could feel her celebrating with me at each discharge.

Mary is my "go to gal" for everything. She is a queen, but not one placed on a throne, out of the reach of those who need her. I've tried my hardest to share this devotion with my children. We pray daily rosaries and weave flower crowns every May. When awoken by nightmares, my children are often reminded to ask for Our Lady's help in getting back to sleep; as their heavenly mother, she doesn't want them to be scared, either!

As I entered the Church, with only a basic knowledge of the faith, I could never have imagined how my relationship with Mary would grow and sustain me. In hindsight, I can see how God's hand was leading me closer to her. Now she is not only Queen of Heaven and Earth, but of our home as well, next to her son, Christ our King.

Mary, Queen of Heaven and Earth, pray for us.

Afterword

The events in the life and motherhood of Mary are extraordinary. Yet, her holiness doesn't just consist in those extraordinary moments. It consists in each small moment of immense love—in the dishes she washed, the meals she cooked, the lessons she taught her little Son. Her holiness consists in the little moments.

If this is true for Mary, how much more so is it true for us? If we enter into these little moments, inspired by the love of Mary we, too, can become saints.

Mary, Queen of All Saints and Queen of Mothers, pray for us.

Acknowledgements

Thank you, first and foremost, to the amazing women who contributed to this volume. Frannie, Haley, Jenny, Caitlyn, Cari, Katie, Mary, Amy, Morgan, Christy, Kate, Katie, Dwija, Jenna, Mary Helen, and Kelly it has been an absolute joy and privilege to work with each of you on this project. I have never enjoyed proofreading a manuscript as much as I have this one! You are all such beautiful mothers and godmothers, and I thank you for sharing the beauty of your vocation with all of us. A special thanks to Amy Garro, for her beautiful photography, which is featured throughout the book.

A thank you, too, to all the spouses who entertained little ones so that these reflections could be written. Thank you to Alec, Daniel, David, Jon, Ken, John, Jerry, John, Joseph, Paul, Brian, Tomas, Mike, Nate, Tony, and, of course, my own dear Andrew. Behind every holy woman is a St. Joseph, and you are ours. Thank you for your love and support!

A thank you, too, to all the little ones who let their mommies get this writing done. Your sacrifice is greatly appreciated. Thank you, too, for teaching your mothers and godmothers so much. You are each a gift! A special thank you to my beautiful little Therese and Maria, for helping me along to heaven. I love you, my sweethearts.

Thank you to my own mother, to whom this book is dedicated. Mom, I was (and am) inspired by your incredible love for Mary. Thank you for sharing that special devotion with me, and for teaching me how to be a mother by your own beautiful example.

A final thank you to our Heavenly Mother, by whose intercession I am daily sustained. I love you, dear Mother.

Our Lady of Mount Carmel, pray for us.

About the Authors

Michele E. Chronister (editor and contributor) is a mother to two and godmother to three. She has published two books with Liguori Publications: *Handbook for Adaptive Catechesis* and *Faith Beginnings*. She has also contributed to *Catholic Digest,* the *Catechetical Leader,* and is a regular contributor for *Ignitum Today.* She blogs at "My Domestic Monastery" (www.mydomesticmonastery.com), a blog designed to encourage and inspire other Catholic families as they work to build a culture of faith in their homes.

Contributors:

Dwija Borobia is a mother of six (with one in heaven). She is the author of "House Unseen, Life Unscripted" (www.houseunseen.com) where she blogs about her experiences as a Catholic homeschooling mom and convert.

Katie Busch is a mother to two little girls. She homeschools her oldest and is a graduate of the University of Notre Dame, where she studied theology.

Caitlyn Buttaci is a mother to two and godmother to one. She is an accountant and the author of the blog "Harvesting Home" (http://harvestinghome.blogspot.com) where she reflects on her faith and life as a working mother and wife to a doctoral student.

Morgan Caudle is a mother to four little ones on earth and one in heaven. She is also a godmother and author of the blog "Fabrics and Fun" (www.fabricsandfun.wordpress.com), a blog about Catholic mothering.

Cari Donaldson - A mother of six, Cari is a homeschooler, a Catholic convert, and the author of the popular *Pope Awesome and Other Stories*. She shares her thoughts and stories on her blog, "Clan Donaldson" (http://clan-donaldson.com).

Amy Garro is a mother of three. She blogs regularly at "Go Forth and Mother" (www.goforthandmother.com), as well at her successful quilting blog "13 Spools" (www.13spools.com). She is the coauthor of Liguori's *Faith Beginnings*, and a godmother to one.

Jenna Hines is a mother to two little ones, and proud owner of the Etsy business "Call Her Happy" and shares her experiences and inspiration as a Catholic mother on her blog that bears the same name (http://callherhappy.com).

Christy Isinger is a mother of five, and hails from chilly Canada. She shares her insights on the beauty and importance of cultivating the home (as well as other funny and insightful thoughts) over at "Fountains of Home" (http://fountainsofhome.blogspot.com).

Mary Lenaburg is mother to two adult children (one of whom is now in heaven), as well as godmother to nine. She blogs at the popular Catholic blog "Passionate Perseverance" (www.passionateperseverance.blogspot.com) as well as being an occasional contributor for the blog "Fine Linen and Purple" (www.finelinenandpurple.com), a lifestyle blog for Catholic women.

Kelly Mantoan is a homeschool teacher and mother of five (including two little boys who are non-ambulatory). She's a blogger and speaker, and recently published *The Best Laid Plans.* She shares her wit and wisdom over at "This Ain't the Lyceum" (http://thisaintthelyceum.org)

Kate Mattoon is an elementary school teacher. She has two goddaughters, Brittany (age 9), and Enmy (age 14). Both girls live in Honduras. She became their godmother while living and serving as a missionary/teacher at the Catholic orphanage ("The Farm of the Child," http://www.farmofthechild.org) where Brittany lives, and Enmy goes to school.

Frannie Moen is a mother of one, who recently completed her MA in Theology from Saint Louis University. She has written for The Philadelphia Inquirer, National Catholic Register, and The Foundry. She currently works for the Knights of Columbus and maintains the
blog for the Blessed John Paul II shrine.

Katie Schulte is a mother to two little ones on earth (and one in heaven). Katie earned her MA in Theology through the University of Notre Dame. She is also a graduate of Notre Dame's ECHO program for catechetical leader formation.

Haley Stewart is a mother of three. She blogs regularly at her popular Catholic blog "Carrots for Michaelmas" (www.carrotsformichaelmas.com). She and her husband also co-wrote the book *Feast! Real Food, Reflections, and Simple Living for the Christian Year* and its sequel *More Feasts!* She has also written contributions for Catholic Exchange, BlogHer, and AltCatholicah.

Jenny Uebbing is a mother of three (with one on the way), who blogs regularly at "Mama Needs Coffee" (www.mamaneedscoffee.com) and has also written for Our Sunday Visitor, Catholic Exchange, and Catholic News Agency. Jenny is also the content editor for Heroic News (www.heroicnews.org).

Mary Helen Wofford is a mother of two who took up running as a way to raise money and awareness when her oldest child was diagnosed with two rare disorders. She shares her running adventures and perspectives on family and home over at "A Helping of Home" (http://ahelpingofhome.blogspot.com).

45385869R00103

Made in the USA
Lexington, KY
25 September 2015